Mark Brocklesb

RECORDING SOUND

A CONCISE GUIDE TO
THE ART OF RECORDING

Mark Brocklesby

RECORDING SOUND

A CONCISE GUIDE TO
THE ART OF RECORDING

 THE CROWOOD PRESS

CONTENTS

PREFACE

It has been suggested that a great mix is more than just balancing, blending and placing sounds within the listening soundstage. The process of mixing and the act of being creative with a given mix are perhaps two different schools of thought. In my view, and many practitioners would agree, in many respects the latter is more akin to telling a story.

If we consider a mix as being similar to telling a story, then 'once upon a time' can often be the recording process for many artists and practitioners. However, it is also fair to state that in some circumstances recording may be the only process involved from inception to the final listener, so in this instance it also has to be akin to the 'happy ever after' scenario.

To say I have always loved recording and my role as a recording engineer is a huge understatement. I have memories of using tape cassettes and different hi-fi systems to superimpose sounds from one system on the other, and the idea of layering sounds to create something similar to painting a picture that the listener could imagine or re-imagine when it was reproduced had me hooked from the outset.

I would gently suggest that at times there is also a responsibility that comes with recording. It can, for example, act as a historical record and memory. I was recently involved in remastering an album I had helped to produce on its initial release some years ago, since when one of the players, a well-respected musician in the community and a recognisable voice on the radio, has sadly passed away. Hearing his voice again at the start of one of the tracks was a nice, albeit sad experience. It made me feel that the work carried additional value, at least from an emotive perspective.

The recording of the musician in question playing harp alongside another friend, still thankfully very much with us today, playing nylon string acoustic guitar in my old living room in Liverpool was not my best work on many levels. However, it captured a mood, an energy, a spirit, a moment in time and what I believe to be a special performance between two very good musicians.

It was an honour to be there and many memories of that time in my life flooded back after listening again to the recording. I truly love recording for a plethora of reasons, but I find bearing witness to the birth of a performance and how a room's acoustics becomes part of the sound picture being created is something truly special.

I genuinely hope that my enthusiasm and passion for capturing sound has rubbed off on my clients and students over the years and this constitutes one of the main reasons I agreed to write this book.

My love of working with different microphones, preamps and outboard equipment, and what is often termed a 'signal chain' when these are combined in an attempt to create something akin to a picture of sound, albeit imagined, has not diminished, nor has my enjoyment of experimenting with various spaces with interesting acoustics to help craft a production aesthetic, add colour, character and depth (dimension and value) to a recorded sound or sounds, as the case may be.

For over 25 years I have been lucky enough to work on both sides of the glass (in the live room and the control room), recording and performing in various studios. Whether on location, in a project studio or working at a larger studio facility, I can honestly say that being a recordist, a recording engineer tasked with capturing sound, is my favourite part of the record production process.

I am not embarrassed to admit there have been moments when the idea of 'getting goosebumps' is genuinely less of a cliché and more of a testament to really loving what I do. If this book serves to inspire even one person to go out and record an interesting sound, a space, a unique performance, or to document a moment in time, then I will see this book as a success.

INTRODUCTION

Recording is in part an art, and I have long held the belief, rightly or wrongly, that expressing yourself is not a competition and therefore I do not measure its results, or rather think in terms of something being better or worse. Through this lens, at least, it is more a case of what moves and inspires you when it comes to the artistic aspect of capturing sound. I like to believe that we all express ourselves differently. Indeed, when it comes to choosing what to record there are no rules.

For example, I often enjoy routing different sounds, acoustic or otherwise, through various types of speakers and then experiment by placing objects on these speakers. Whether the sounds are pre-recorded or being generated live there and then, the speakers can be used to make various acoustic instruments and objects resonate. This acoustic excitation can take a fairly average sound and help to sculpt something that sounds interesting.

When such sounds are recorded, it can open up a plethora of creative possibilities. This signal flow and process, which utilises in part the technique of re-amping, is one of many techniques that will be addressed as the book progresses, but in essence this is arguably recording applied in a very creative manner and the results in some instances could be considered as suitable and a complementary form of sound design for a given brief.

Though the art of recording and taking the time to experiment can be extremely enjoyable and often rewarding, there are standards, formats and theoretical principles that underpin good practice, and this is something we will look at over the coming chapters: the science behind the art.

Having stated this, perhaps it would be good to begin by saying what this book is and what it is not. It is aimed at beginners and hobbyists, but ideally I hope it will also be a useful reference guide for those practitioners who may consider themselves as semi-professional. My intention is to introduce the reader to the theory and practice associated with recording in a manner that is not overwhelming, cold or discouraging.

I will use anecdotes from industry colleagues, friends and my own personal experiences to discuss the art and practice, hoping, perhaps more pertinently, to humanise the process and dispel some of the common misnomers associated with capturing sound.

It will be necessary to throw in some relevant and appropriate terminology throughout (although I hope the glossary will provide some explanation). This is not intended to sound clever. As I often tell my students, it is in part through learning the language of the practitioner that we can better understand one another. Even if it is just the basics, such knowledge and language can go a long way towards breaking down barriers and working towards shared values and standards associated with what is considered good practice.

Whenever I go on holiday and visit a non-English speaking country I will always try to learn the basics of the language native to where I am staying. I have always felt that not only do I feel better about myself (although perhaps that is just me), but that people appreciate and respect you for trying. My experience working with students and clients is no different. Whether in the studio or on location the recordings have always benefited in many ways from shared knowledge, not least in a creative manner.

I also want to redress that recording is in its own right a very specific art and discipline. This is not a criticism of modern production or how various stakeholders and practitioners identify a specific role within the process of making a record. It is simply to suggest that recording, mixing and mastering are all very different processes and, from recent experience at least, these separate disciplines tend to get mixed up and bundled into one process from time to time.

There are crossover points in terms of techniques, methodology and processing. Editing, for example, whether applied in a corrective or creative manner, can be utilised in all three of these distinct and arguably specialised stages.

Many thought processes, workflows and styles of practice can provoke debate. Some practitioners, for example, now apply techniques and processing to a stage of making a record that was previously associated with other specific stages, such as when processing associated with the arguably modern concept of mastering is applied at the mixing stage: I say modern because mastering was at one time primarily more focused on formatting the final product.

What works for one practitioner may be frowned upon by another and, depending on the genre and style of project, there are multiple factors to consider and ways of working to achieve a specified outcome.

Indeed, one of the many things I intend to do is not to get bogged down with semantics in relation to the job requirements or methods of other practitioners. This book is going to focus purely on recording.

This book is not a substitute for informed research or further study. It is an overview and hopefully a catalyst, a springboard if you please, towards starting a journey of discovery. My hope is that it will inspire its readers to get out and record various sounds. With the improvement of digital signal processing (DSP) and access to more affordable equipment, there has arguably never been a time less restrictive when it comes to capturing sound.

When it comes to capturing a good recording, my advice would be that you should concentrate on building up a store of knowledge that can be applied as needed:

1. Take time to learn the basic theory and practice (including the personnel, various practitioners and stakeholders) associated with recording. Be consistent in the standard of relevant knowledge you need to acquire to help underpin decision making, rather than relying on the occasional happy accident that might occur. A common suggestion is that 'if it sounds good, it is good'. I don't disagree with this sentiment

but, whether a hobbyist or professional, it is good to know how to recreate your greatest sounding recordings for continuity at the very least. In order to achieve this I would suggest that you undertake additional research and reading, and when starting out on your journey try to focus your attention on the following:

- The basic principles of 'acoustics' (the science of sound or how a particular environment impacts upon a given sound within a particular space) and 'psychoacoustics' (how we perceive and respond to audio, or more specifically auditory stimuli, focusing on what happens between sound arriving at the ear and it being transmitted to and processed via the brain);
- Microphone types (operating principles and design);
- Microphone techniques (mono, stereo and multichannel arrays);
- Microphone placement and the listening soundstage;
- The signal chain or, as it is sometimes known, signal flow;
- Gain staging. This is in part the process by which the sound or sounds being captured are amplified to a usable level. Here a practitioner, for example, considers the signal to noise ratio (SNR) and the headroom of a signal. However, this can also be considered a very creative stage since, depending on the equipment being utilised in the signal chain, colour, tone, harmonic resonance and overtones can be added to the sound being captured.

2. Have a vision. Listen to reference tracks and storyboard what you are trying to achieve in terms of the overall production aesthetic. Above all else, try to enjoy the process and, where possible, take your time. Practise, experiment and work with a wide variety of sound sources, styles and musical genres in a variety of spaces.
3. Build upon the basic foundations laid out in this book. This should be achieved by investing time to undertake further study, research and practice.

There is something special about the process and art of recording that is more than just about capturing a sound or a given moment in time, a quality that may be described as organic.

Examining a human performance in detail, for example, taking time to analyse and celebrate all the imperfections and inconsistencies associated with playing an instrument and using the human voice to create a musical experience, will reveal something that is arguably unique. As I often tell my students, some of my favourite records are far from perfect.

I guess we can always debate the limitations and potential pitfalls, and ultimately run the risk of pigeonholing or backing ourselves into a proverbial corner, when attempting to state what constitutes perfection in anything, let alone record production.

Once again, however, rightly or wrongly I find the word is occasionally associated with some modern production tools and techniques when discussing the subject with my students – especially modern tools that can be used for tuning and timing.

My point is that recording in its purest application captures a performance in its natural state, including all the mistakes, and there is something human about this in terms of dynamics and feel. There is also something to said about the way sound is affected in terms of the acoustics within a given space. Again, when one contemplates the randomness of diffuse (uncorrelated) sound there is an aspect of chaos added to a recorded performance in terms of sound waves propagating (transmitting or moving) through a space.

Recording is in some ways an honest process when you look at it from this perspective. Unlike other stages in record production, you do not have to be fixated with staring at a screen and obsessing with the tiniest of edits in order to correct a given sound.

Of course I do recognise, and hope it goes without saying, that when working with musicians and artists playing live it is better to capture the best performance possible and this alone involves many contributing factors. I am not saying, though, that practices such as recording don't come without their own set of concerns and aspects to become fixated on.

In regards to how room acoustics colour and alter a given sound source, factors such as room reflections, standing waves, and the reverberation characteristic of a given space, can add character to a recording and ultimately a production as a whole (not always favorably).

Whether something sounds good or bad is a matter of taste when it comes to experimenting with recording in various environments.

This book is solely focused on the role of the recording engineer and recording as an art and discipline in its own right. There is no doubt that the various different roles involved within the record production process share some similarities, both in terms of applied theory and practice. Nevertheless, for the sake of clarity I feel it would be prudent to discuss briefly the basic roles and responsibilities of the other stakeholders and practitioners associated with record production. Skilled engineers working with audio also undertake other tasks, of course, such as those who specialise in electronics, developing many of the tools to which we have become accustomed, but that is beyond the range of this book.

You have most likely heard of recording engineers, mix engineers, mastering engineers and assistant engineers. Each of these engineers or specialists, bar the assistant, is normally but not exclusively focused on a very specific discipline, which in turn is associated with specific roles and practices, some of which identify with extremely specialist techniques and delivery systems.

Mastering engineers can, for example, be tasked with cutting to vinyl, half speed or otherwise, and this process has its own set of considerations, including EQ curves, that need to be addressed in order to do the best job possible when translating a finished mix from, most commonly today, a digital format to an analogue, mechanical format.

Some mastering engineers are responsible for restoring old recordings, transferring older sessions for storage and archiving purposes and for remastering. This often includes using old tape machines and other formats and therefore requires specialist knowledge.

Recording engineers working on location have to take into account a different set of factors to those working in a recording studio, such as further understanding of certain principles associated with acoustics. Whereas a recording studio often has treatment to control and sometimes manipulate the sound (acoustics) of a live room (a space for recording housed in the facility), location recordists do not always have the assurance that where they are recording has the same amount of control. In turn certain spaces may present a whole set of problems in relation to how a given sound source will be affected by the acoustic characteristics of the environment in which the practitioners find themselves working.

Recording engineers may be expected to record using techniques and arrays of microphones to capture sound in a manner that is intended to be utilised in a spatial audio or surround sound playback format. This requires the engineer to apply very specialist knowledge in order to work towards a specific brief. The same could be said of mix engineers, whether they are mixing for stereo, surround or other spatial audio delivery systems and formats.

The role of the assistant fluctuates depending on the type of session – recording, mixing or mastering – and the needs of the head engineer.

As briefly touched upon earlier, there are roles and practices that cross over between the different engineering disciplines, such as editing. Whether applied in a corrective (fixing things) or creative manner (normally adding or taking away in order to enhance production), editing can arguably be applied at any point during the chain of events that constitutes the record production process.

We will look at how editing is relevant to the recording process, or more specifically the role of a recording engineer, in the final chapter. All I will say for now is that traditionally, unless otherwise agreed, the recording engineer would be expected to apply any corrective editing in order to get a project ready for the mix engineer. This, though, is only relevant if a mix engineer is required.

Many recording engineers would suggest that a great recording, genre specific, mixes itself and that after suitable microphones have been placed appropriately it is a simple case of balancing and placing the recorded sounds within the listening soundstage.

This is one of the many perks of having access to a great-sounding studio with a decent microphone collection. Studios with well-considered acoustic treatment assist a practitioner in two main ways. Firstly, in a well-designed control room (the room that houses the engineer and recording equipment such as a mixing console, computer and outboard) the engineer can trust what they hear coming from the speakers, and not be worried that the listening environment is being unfavourably coloured by the sound of the room itself via various standing waves (see Glossary) and room reflections.

Similarly, if a live room is treated to control the reverberation characteristic (see Glossary), setting up and placing microphones does not present as many challenges as may arise when working with potentially problematic or unwanted room resonances, although that is arguably one of the more rewarding challenges of working on location or in an environment that has an interesting sound.

THE LISTENING SOUNDSTAGE

When discussing the soundstage in this book, I am not referring to the creation of a specific facility designed for film sound and post-production. In this instance the listening soundstage is concerned with how the listener hears a recorded sound when reproduced over either speakers or headphones. There is some excellent work by Michael Williams in his two-volume *Microphone Arrays for Stereo and Multichannel Sound Recording* (2004), in which he discusses recording techniques in relation to the creation of virtual sound images, something we will touch upon in Chapter 3.

William Moylan has also published some very interesting and insightful literature, such as his conference paper 'Considering Space in Music', published in the *Journal on the Art of Record Production* (2009), in which he discusses the overall soundstage in relation to dimension and the 'Perceived Performance

Environment'. The individual sound sources within that environment are then considered in terms of location, size and the character of the sound based on the environment. This is something that you should consider in more detail as the book progresses, taking acoustics and psychoacoustics into account.

Acoustics can be considered as the science of sound and the effect a physical space has on a sound generated within that given space. Psychoacoustics is concerned with how we perceive sound when reacting to an auditory stimulus. The latter ties in nicely with the more general interpretation of the listening soundstage, one where it is concerned with the listener conjuring up a three-dimensional space in which all the sound sources can be placed. This can be confusing for many starting out as recording engineers.

From a literal perspective stereo playback, over two speakers for example, only deals with the horizontal plane. It is essentially two-dimensional, so why are we discussing a listening soundstage that has three dimensions?

This is where perception and psychoacoustics play a part. To be fair engineers will often manipulate the listening soundstage during the mixing stage by applying a mixture of spectral (such as EQ, distortion or other tonal processing), spatial (reverberation, echo and delays) and dynamic processing (compression and expansion) to exaggerate, manipulate and control the localisation of a reproduced sound.

The listening soundstage can generally be seen as the perceived placement of sound sources and their size within a given environment from left to right, front to back and top to bottom. Note that the last of these is related to perception unless specific recording and microphone techniques and playback requirements, including speaker configurations, for example, are taken into consideration.

Next time you listen back to any recording try to picture each sound you can hear as a shape. Where does that shape live within the artificial cube we have just described? Where is it placed in terms of the left and right speaker? Is it in the forefront or background, and does it sound as if it is lifting out of the recording or does it sit right in the centre?

Though this book is focused on recording, it is worth taking a look at David Gibson's book *The Art of Mixing: A Visual Guide to Recording, Engineering and Production* (Routledge, 2018). This offers a great visual representation of where various sounds may sit within the artificial cube we have just touched upon and which we will refer to as the 'listening soundstage'.

In relation to the listening soundstage, when listening to recordings over two or more speakers we are often able to close our eyes and picture a sound or sounds between or around the speakers. In such circumstances it is akin to having another speaker. This is referred to as a 'phantom image', not in the sense of a ghost haunting your recordings, but rather of an illusion.

With a little know-how, good recording technique and tasteful, measured processing during editing and mixing can enhance these phantom images and add a sense of realism to the listening soundstage. At this point we could also consider manipulating the listening soundstage in order to move away from a sense of realism, but that is a whole other book.

It is also worth mentioning that the listening soundstage in terms of a finished mixed and mastered product is not static. Sounds are dynamic, and there is movement. Dynamics can be considered as more than just the difference between quiet and loud phrases or moments in an arrangement. There is also a concept of spatial dynamics.

As was suggested earlier, mixes are often akin to telling a story in which movement and dynamic changes in tone, level and space convey a sense of drama and emotion. When considering recording and how sound is reproduced we are not always dealing with stereophonic sound, and so discussing it in terms of a listening soundstage can be a more open-ended way to picture the size and placement of a given sound beyond the stereo image to which many of us are accustomed. Arguably, however, a well-considered speaker set-up for stereophonic playback in a treated space or room with favourable acoustics can generate all sorts of perceived images that can appear to transcend a sense of depth and width.

1
AN INTRODUCTION TO MICROPHONES

Sound is both a sensation associated with the scientific school of psychoacoustics and a stimulus (acoustics and physics). The former is associated with how we perceive sound when it reaches our ears, the latter is arguably more of an obvious concern when it comes to the literal side of capturing sound as it pertains to sound as a wave motion within different mediums, such as how sound waves propagate within air.

Specialist microphones such as hydrophones are used to capture sound travelling through other elastic mediums, such as water. Here, however, we will be focusing on how microphones are used in several ways to capture and take a reading of the change in air pressure caused by an acoustic instrument, the human voice or any other device used to create and amplify what we ultimately hear as a sound worth recording.

The air pressure in the immediate vicinity is disturbed every time we open our mouths to speak, hit a drum or pluck the string on a guitar. Though technically the air is never at rest, an action such as hitting a drum will disturb the air molecules in a manner similar to the motion of a spring. The air does not move, rather the molecules will oscillate, or in more simple terms vibrate backwards and forwards, like a spring, disturbing the air molecules around them.

This basic disturbance between a point of rest or equilibrium and the subsequent inertia of air molecules moving backwards and forwards is considered as a simple harmonic motion and often visualised as a sine wave.

This motion of the air molecules oscillating is periodic and sound waves are generally measured in how many cycles a second these periodic displacements of the air molecules take place per second. These cycles are measured in Hertz (Hz) and the resulting figure is often referred to as the frequency. At this stage it is worth noting that frequency, an objective measurement of a periodic signal, and pitch, a subjective expression based on the perception of a tone, are very different.

There are many other comparable or analogous factors that are in reality very different when it comes to understanding sound, such as loudness and intensity. The former is considered a sensation and is again very subjective. In reality, understanding sound is a complex subject and there are many aspects to consider.

Sound propagation pertains in part to the compression and rarefaction (high and low pressure) of the oscillating air molecules as they vibrate backwards and forwards. However, it is also related to how sound waves travel and are altered by a given space. This subject is something we will be considering in terms of how the acoustics of a given space can impact upon the choices a recording engineer makes when approaching capturing a sound or performance.

If you are interested in undertaking further reading and learning more about the science of sound and how we perceive sound, I would highly recommend reading F. Alton Everest and Ken C. Pohlmann's *Master Handbook of Acoustics* (McGraw Hill, 7th edn 2021).

WHAT IS A MICROPHONE?

Whether recording an orchestra, wheelie bins as percussion instruments or capturing the sound of seagulls for a song while sitting on the roof of a studio at the request of an artist – yes, this happened – capturing sound in the acoustic domain, the natural world or, more specifically in relation to lots of modern production approaches, 'outside of the box' generally requires the use of some sort of microphone.

A common factor that links all microphones, even though they come in many shapes and sizes, boasting varied specifications and characteristics that can help inform our decision making when approaching capturing a given acoustic sound source, is that they work by converting one source of energy into another. A change in air pressure or more simply, a variation in sound pressure taking place in the vicinity of a microphone's diaphragm, creates a measurable, though minute, alternating voltage. A microphone is in essence a transducer.

How this change in air pressure is converted into a measurable change in voltage, effectively attempting to mirror the original pressure changes taking place within the vicinity of a given sound source, varies depending on the operating principle of the given microphone. There are three main types of microphones that you are most likely come across when recording:

- Condenser (capacitor) microphones, sometimes referred to as 'true' or 'electret' condenser microphones
- Dynamic (moving coil) microphones
- Ribbon microphones.

All of these types come in different shapes, sizes and styles of encasing, for example, offering a wide variety of options in terms of specifications, and how these may influence a practitioner's decision-making is something we will look at in later chapters.

I often hear people refer to microphones as resembling the human ear, especially when discussing how various microphones hear different tones. Microphones indeed have very individual 'frequency responses', which is simply how a microphone responds to a given frequency or, more accurately, frequencies within the agreed human hearing range of 20Hz to 20kHz. These frequency responses alternate depending on various factors and this can work in a practitioner's favour depending on the application, something that will again become more apparent as we progress.

I would suggest, however, that it is misleading to compare microphones to the human ear. Unless specialist considerations are taken into account when setting up for recording and playback, microphones alone do not generally provide the listener with a sense of realism in terms of capturing a natural soundstage.

Many of the colleagues I have been fortunate to work with have always preferred the idea that microphones are more like different drawing tools or paintbrushes, especially when we associate tone with colour and the recording medium becomes the canvas on which we are painting. Does that mean a recordist or recording engineer should ask themselves what is it they are trying to paint?

Placing just any microphone in front of a given sound source will not capture the audio in a manner that allows the listener to hear the same sound as one would hear it in the natural world or attain a true sense of realism.

Stereo microphone techniques can provide decent localisation in terms of where a given sound source is placed within the listening sound stage. Such recordings can provide a sense of width and depth, but for a more realistic, natural-sounding recording the recordist must take periphony, sound with height, into consideration.

If we understand this from the outset, then how a practitioner utilises a microphone is more down to personal taste. Do we like the sound we have captured or not? Does it sound good on the record and is the sound you have captured suitable for the production aesthetic you are trying to attain as a whole?

The production aesthetic in this sense is simply the overall mood or style of sound you are trying to emulate or create. One example of a production aesthetic is that some recordings sound very intimate and close, whereas others are very open, expansive or possibly even distant. There are, of course, increments in between and recordings that mix various techniques and create hybrid soundstages by blending many different recorded environments. In regard to the latter, a recording engineer working in different environments should also consider how sound will be altered and coloured based on the acoustics of the space they are working in, taking into account its 'reverberation characteristic' (see Glossary).

A good place to start with any microphone is to experiment with its placement. Again, this is something we will look at in more detail in later chapters, but for now let us simplify how a microphone can be positioned in relation to the sound source you wish to capture. The microphone will either be placed close to a given sound source (sometimes referred to as direct positioning) or placed at a distance (sometimes called ambient). Of course, that is fairly vague and I would suggest that you start by wearing a pair of headphones and experiment by placing the microphone either close to the sound source or at a distance. Move the microphone until you like what you hear and try to identify what is it you particularly like about the sound you are recording.

I must admit, however, that many professional practitioners struggle to articulate verbally what it is they like about a specific sound, at least in what can be considered a universal language. You will often hear engineers and producers refer to a sound being dark or having lift, air, sparkle and so on. Delving into the language associated with describing sound, though, could be a whole other book.

One microphone alone can capture a sense of depth. Indeed, a single microphone from a distance will allow the listener to gauge the size of the space you are recording in to a certain degree. Localising where a sound source is placed within that given space is a different matter entirely and requires stereographic information within the recorded signal.

Although stereo recording, localisation and stereophonic/stereographic images will be covered in the next chapter, for now I would recommend listening to the recordings posted on YouTube in the excellent 'OneMic – the minimalist recording series' in which, as the title infers, a stereo microphone is set up in a room with controlled or interesting, usable acoustics. The musicians are all provided with the exact same headphone mix (foldback) and either the musicians themselves or the recording engineers position the performers in a manner that acts as a fader and a panner. The former depends on how upfront and loud the performers are within the listening soundstage, while the latter relates to where they are positioned in terms of where the sources can be heard from left to right.

More of this will make sense when we discuss various techniques and examine the basic theoretical concepts that underpin such practice.

Most people arguably still listen in mono or mainly stereo when it comes to ingesting music alone, so I will focus on methodology, techniques and thinking based on that premise.

We will look in more detail at how we hear, measure and process sound in Chapter 4 as such considerations can be helpful in understanding how and why various techniques are used by a given practitioner when approaching a particular type of recording.

For now, let's take a look at how sound works and how microphones operate and function in the process of capturing sound.

Modern recording can be broken up into three principal stages: the physical, the electrical and the digital. When recording the human voice or an acoustic instrument, for example, the first stage involves the given sound source or sources being able to disturb the pressure of the medium in which it is being situated. For the most part this is air (as opposed to water, for example) and therefore we are dealing with a change in air pressure, kinetic energy more specifically, and to convert this type of energy into an energy that we can control and harness in a more practical way the microphone, a mechanical device, acts as a transducer converting a change in pressure to a variable electrical current. Once we have the reading of a sound source as an electrical signal, we can amplify the signal and re-route it via cables to various electrical devices for a plethora of reasons, one of which is to digitise the electrical signals via converters.

Converters have two primary functions: to convert an analogue signal (namely the electrical) to digital (AD stage) '1s' and zeros', and then the digital back to analogue (DA stage).

To return to the initial change in air pressure, when you hit a drum, pluck a guitar string or indeed use your voice box and mouth to create sound you are disturbing the pressure of the air in that vicinity. The form of energy you are creating a disturbance within is technically referred to as 'confined kinetic energy'.

Depending on how loud the sound is, or rather how much sound pressure is generated by a given source, will have impact on how loud we hear and in turn perceive a sound source to be.

Room acoustics, or how a room sounds and impacts upon a said sound in simpler terms, will also change in part due to these sound pressure levels (SPLs).

The higher the SPL generated by a sound source the more the environment where the sound source is housed will colour the original sound. Higher SPLs increase the excitation of an environment as sound reflects, refracts and diffracts (see Glossary).

The human ear detects these often hugely dynamic changes in air pressure from the most minute through to the larger and ultimately louder disturbances. How we measure these changes can easily become very complex and this is something I am keen to avoid.

Indeed, it is not just the changes in air pressure at the human ear that some researchers are interested in when looking at modern audio production, mapping out and emulating a variety of listening experiences. Hearing is also concerned with localising from where a sound source is coming. It is not just concerned with how loud a given sound source is but also where the sound source is emanating from.

Sound pressure is measured in Pascals. The human ear can detect vast differences when it comes to these changes in pressure, but from the sound engineer's perspective such large-scale incremental changes and variations, especially when one looks at micropascals, are not a practical way to measure and manipulate how loud a given signal is or needs to be. Therefore the decibel can be used to compare various sources of power in a smaller and more user-friendly manner, a logarithmic scale.

When dealing with confined kinetic energy, the changes or disturbance in air pressure generated by hitting a drum, for example, an engineer can work with the dB SPL (sound pressure level) scale.

Whereas the human ear has the ear drum and interconnecting parts to detect and read changes in air pressure, microphones use some form of lightweight, usually metallic-coated diaphragm or ribbon to respond to changes in SPLs.

As the human ear takes the physical changes detected in air pressure and converts them in part to neurological pulses, ear to brain stimuli, a microphone acts as a transducer. Using some sort of diaphragm or ribbon, it takes a reading of the change in air pressure, or more precisely variations in sound pressure at the diaphragm of a microphone, and depending on the operating principle converts the changes into measurable change in voltage.

Once the measurable signal is electrical other dB scales can be used. You can then work with the electrical signal to amplify it to usable levels, divert it to other electrical tools and send it to converters to be digitised.

OPERATING PRINCIPLES

CONDENSER MICROPHONES

Condenser microphones utilise a fixed back plate and a diaphragm to form a capacitor. The diaphragm can be constructed using a very thin lightweight polymer or any conductive material that can be polarised with a small electrical charge.

These capacitor microphones are either pre-powered electret condensers or condensers that require a DC biased external power source.

When a change in air pressure takes place in the vicinity of the condenser microphone the fixed back plate and polarised diaphragm act as the opposing sides of a capacitor and the lightweight diaphragm moves backwards and forwards in sympathy with the alternating, incoming pressure level. This movement alters the capacitance and creates a change in voltage to mirror the original variations in sound pressure.

This changing voltage can then be amplified to a usable signal and in modern systems is digitised via converters. The reverse of this is when the signal leaves the converters at the DA stage and the digital signal is converted back into a changing voltage. This changing voltage is then used to drive speaker cones and diaphragms backwards and forwards to disturb the air pressure in the vicinity of the speaker or headphone driver, and in turn the changes in pressure arrive at our ears and pass stimuli to the brain. This is a very simplified account, but nevertheless to this day I think the whole process is nothing short of magic!

You can reasonably suggest that microphones are in essence speakers in reverse. Though with modern design and technological considerations there are variations, for the most part large diaphragm microphones are better at capturing low frequencies, just as large speakers are used to recreate low frequencies. If you do not have access to the specifications of a given microphone, it is not unusual to look at the size of the diaphragm to make an educated guess as to whether it would be suitable for recording a given sound source in relation to where that sound sits within the frequency spectrum, although there is of course more to consider here.

DYNAMIC MICROPHONES (MOVING COILS)

Dynamic microphones do not require any sort of power, unlike capacitor microphones. Moving coil, dynamic microphones generate their own variation in voltage by acting as mini electrical generators. More specifically they utilise the principle of 'electromagnetic induction'. In this instance the diaphragm housed within a dynamic microphone is attached to a small metal wire coil positioned within a magnetic field. When a change in sound pressure takes place in the vicinity of the microphone's diaphragm, the coil attached to the diaphragm moves backwards and forwards within a permanent magnet. Such movement between the north and south pole of the magnet generates a voltage that varies in response to the original changes in sound pressure. The attached coil, however, can physically limit the movement of the diaphragm and in turn restrict the ability to capture high frequencies within the agreed audible frequency range of human hearing as well as ultrasound, hypersonics and harmonics that are outside the range.

The low-level voltage generated by dynamic microphones generally requires more amplification and therefore in terms of signal to noise ratio, discussed in the next chapter, they are not ideal for capturing sounds at a distance.

Many practitioners, however, like dynamics for a number of reasons. They are mostly affordable, well-built and hard-wearing microphones that can cope with very high sound pressure levels and therefore can be placed up close to any given sound source.

RIBBON MICROPHONES

Ribbon microphones use the same electromagnetic induction principle as dynamic, moving coil microphones. However, instead of utilising some form of lightweight diaphragm attached to a metal coil and suspended within a magnetic field, the ribbon itself acts as the diaphragm and ultimately the transducer.

The ribbon is normally made from an extremely lightweight, thin strip of metal such as aluminium. Practitioners love them for their sensitivity and sound. Whereas some condenser microphones can hype and exaggerate the higher mid- and high frequency ranges and in turn sound very bright and occasionally harsh, ribbons are known for sounding more natural and in some cases practitioners allude to them having a darker tone.

Some ribbon microphones are quite delicate and need to be handled with care. At the very least they should be covered well when not in use (as should most microphones) and unless otherwise stated you should avoid sending phantom power down a standard XLR cable. Phantom power, sometimes represented as '+48v', which is used to power some condenser microphones, Direct Inject (DI) boxes and more modern hybrid active ribbon microphones, can damage a standard passive ribbon microphone by stretching and warping the ribbon element itself.

Many modern ribbons have safety features built in, incorporating active elements in the design that require phantom power, or you can buy phantom blockers to protect your microphones.

SENSITIVITY

How well does a given microphone work from a distance? How well will a microphone capture very low volume levels? Will I need to amplify one microphone more than another in order to attain a decent signal level?

All of these questions can be related directly to the sensitivity of a microphone. It can be a nightmare reading a specification chart for the first time, however, so taking time to understand the basics can be beneficial to you as a practitioner.

Sensitivity basically pertains to the output of a microphone in relation to its input. A microphone is a transducer that converts changes in SPLs into changes in voltage. Some microphones generate lower voltage outputs in relation to incoming

SPLs than others and this can be useful in many applications.

Less sensitive microphones may, for example, be far more suitable and less likely to distort when placed very close up (direct microphone positioning) to a sound source that is generating extremely high SPLs. Many practitioners also like to use less sensitive microphones in certain situations as it gives them more headroom when it comes to gain staging (see Chapter 2), which may help to add tone and colour via harmonics induced via various electronic elements such as transformers and valves.

Though there are always exceptions, especially in modern hybrid designs, dynamic microphones are generally less sensitive than condensers and some ribbons.

FREQUENCY RESPONSE

I suggested earlier that microphones are not like ears in the sense that setting one up to record will not yield a result that necessarily sounds natural, real or immersive when reproduced over speakers or headphones. When starting out, however, it is easy to think of a microphone or speaker's frequency response, how it copes with capturing or reproducing soundwaves within the agreed spectrum of human hearing (20Hz–20kHz), as being similar to how it hears a given sound.

Put simply, microphones capture the audible frequencies within the spectrum of 20 cycles per second to 20,000 cycles per second in a different way depending on the microphone. Some microphones have very flat responses, whereas others have enhanced low frequency capture or mid-range boosts that help with the intelligibility of speech, for example.

Some microphones have additional components to further enhance, boost and possibly exaggerate parts of the frequency spectrum. In a simplified fashion this may be considered as an enhancement (boost) or attenuation (cut or shelf)

of frequencies that fall within what is often referred to as low, mid or high range frequencies.

Where a microphone is placed in relation to the direction in which a microphone is most sensitive to a change in air pressure has a direct impact upon how a given microphone responds, or more specifically moving a microphone when utilising certain polar response patterns will change the frequency response of the microphone.

Polar response patterns are concerned with the direction in which a microphone captures sound. Some microphones are directional and to be at their most sensitive they have to be aligned to face a given sound source. When a microphone utilising a directional polar pattern is directly facing a sound source it is said to be 'on axis'. If you move the microphone at any angle from the sound source being captured, then the microphone using a directional polar pattern is said to be 'off axis'.

Positioning a microphone with a directional polar response pattern off axis will alter the frequency response and in turn it can alter the sound of the source being recorded. The first tip when using a microphone with a directional pattern is to play with the axis of the microphone in relation to the sound source being recorded. Use your ears and decide what sounds best for you.

POLAR RESPONSE PATTERNS

Polar response patterns are concerned with the direction in which microphones are most sensitive to sound. The pattern you select, or the patterns required for multi-mono, stereo and multichannel microphone techniques, will have an impact on the direction from which a microphone captures a given sound source.

The two main polar response patterns from which all other polar or 'pickup' patterns are created or crafted are referred to as 'omni' and 'figure of eight'.

When a microphone is set to an 'omni' polar response pattern it is sensitive to SPLs all around

the microphone and is therefore considered to be a non-directional microphone. No matter where you stand around the microphone there is no off-axis position resulting in a drop in sensitivity. Many practitioners feel this yields a more natural sound with a generally flatter frequency response. Microphones utilising an 'omni' pickup pattern are sometimes referred to as 'pressure' microphones. The symbol of a circle you see on some microphones represents the 'omni' polar response/pickup pattern.

A figure of eight pickup pattern, on the other hand, is a bi-directional polar response pattern that is most sensitive and therefore 'on axis' when a sound source is placed directly in front or behind the microphone diaphragm or ribbon. When a microphone uses this pattern either via design or choice – some microphones have variable polar response patterns and allow you to select which pickup pattern to use – there is a lower sensitivity to SPLs arriving at the side of the microphone and this can be very useful. We will look at this in more detail when discussing stereo microphone techniques and tips for recording various instruments and sound sources.

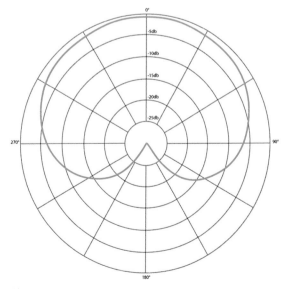

Cardioid polar response pattern.

Large diaphragm condenser microphone with variable polar response patterns (from left to right): omni, cardioid, figure of eight.

Perhaps the most common pickup pattern associated with many microphones is the cardioid pattern created by mixing omni and figure of eight polar response patterns together, or in other design processes by introducing a delay path to the rear of a single diaphragm.

The cardioid polar response pattern is unidirectional, and the symbol used to represent the pattern is shaped like a heart (or a pair of buttocks, if you listen to some of my students). It is most sensitive to capturing sound when the microphone is placed directly in front of the sound source as opposed to at an angle. Sensitivity drops and the frequency response alters when a microphone with such a pattern is angled to face away from an incoming sound source. At 180 degrees, for example. the microphone is said to be 180 degrees 'off axis' and the sensitivity drops to significantly minute values, especially in terms of signal to noise ratio and gain staging.

Variations of cardioid pickup patterns include 'hyper-cardioid', 'super-cardioid' and 'sub-cardioid'.

When using pressure gradient microphones with a bi-directional polar response pattern (figure of eight) or a unidirectional (cardioid, hyper-cardioid and so on), sometimes just referred to as 'directional' microphones, it is possible to alter the frequency response, and in turn the tone, of what you are recording not just by 'on-' and 'off-axis' positioning of the microphone but by moving the microphone closer to a sound source and embracing what is referred to as the 'proximity effect'.

Sometimes known as 'bass tip up', a proximity effect is created when there is a rise in low frequency when a pressure gradient microphone with a directional polar response pattern is placed too close to a source. This is due to the amplitude and phase shift variations occurring at the two sides of the diaphragm. Phase is concerned

Two dynamic microphones, a Shure SM7B and a Sennheiser MD 441, placed 'on axis' to the speaker.

with the time relationship between two signals and is something we will look at in more detail when discussing multi-microphone and stereo recording techniques. Amplitude (*see* Glossary) in this instance refers to the variations in SPLs occurring at both sides of the diaphragm and not the perceived loudness of a signal.

In a practical sense, pressure gradient microphones will emit a noticeably lower frequency response when placed closer to a sound source. This can be useful, for example, for beat boxers shaping sounds from their mouths to sound like bass (kick) drums. It can also benefit those wanting to achieve the more full-bodied sound of a radio presenter or voice-over person, or enhance the performance of bass and baritone vocalists.

Some practitioners like to take advantage of such audible distortions by using the principle on instruments that already generate low frequencies, such as a bass drum, bass amp or upright bass.

The tonal change can be fairly noticeable when using a decent ribbon microphone with a typical figure-of-eight polar response pattern (though be cautious of very high SPLs as this can damage the ribbon).

TRANSIENT RESPONSE

This is directly tied in with some of the specifications we have already discussed, especially frequency response and sensitivity. Transient response is a measurement of how fast or slow a microphone reacts to a given sound source. If a microphone is too quick to respond it can be said to have too much 'overshoot' in relation to its sensitivity and the output of the microphone is disproportionate to its input. This occasionally causes ringing and noticeable sonic artefacts, especially in some basic condensers.

Overshoot is less of an issue in well-designed ribbon microphones. This is partly why so many practitioners feel they have a more natural and less hyped sound than some condenser microphones.

If you want to delve deeper into the specifications of microphones, I recommend reading any of the books written or contributed to by revered engineer John Eargle. There is one more factor to consider before we move on.

IMPEDANCE

This is an important consideration. When applied to microphones or headphones, for example, impedance is the resistance or opposition to the flow of electrical current. All electrical components through which current flows have an amount of resistance to AC. The unit of this resistance is the ohm. Impedance matching occurs when there is the least loss of power between one circuit and another.

For the most part, in practical terms this is no longer something to lose sleep over where microphones are concerned, but I have often found that some of my adjustable preamps with multiple impedance settings can produce different tones, sometimes more apparent than others. On occasions when there has been a notable difference it is often that the microphone sounds as if it was holding back and then opens up.

Impedance mismatches are arguably most noticeable today when using headphones. If you plug a pair of headphones normally used for studio use, which often have a very high impedance rating, for example 250 ohms, into a mobile phone without any further amplification, playback will sound quieter as opposed to using a pair of headphones with a lower impedance rating of say, 32 ohms.

2

RECORDING PRACTICE AND ASSOCIATED CONSIDERATIONS

How you choose to record can have a huge impact on the results you attain. This may seem like a truism, but on occasion I have witnessed practitioners become embroiled in technicalities and leave very little room for actually considering how a recording should best be facilitated.

In one approach musicians can choose, or be instructed, to record together live. Alternatively the recording engineer and artists may opt to record bit by bit, one part at a time, and overdub the layers, piecing the production together and build it from the ground upwards.

There are of course many hybrid approaches. Each style presents its own set of challenges to consider as well as providing numerous potential advantages.

A group of musicians may decide, for example, to record the foundations of a given piece of music as a performance. This could be with or without using a metronome (click) track to help keep time, or indeed with or without headphones and any foldback mix at all. Such a recorded performance can then be enhanced via overdubbing additional layers.

Such an approach to recording, especially if the artists have chosen not to work with a click track, can possibly lead to an issue with feel when it comes to the additional overdubs. This is arguably because one of the many benefits of artists performing together is that they can often lock into one another's playing styles, dynamics, articulation, phrasing and timing. The phenomena loosely associated with a type of symbiotic understanding of one another's playing can be harder to achieve

when individuals or smaller ensembles begin to overdub. This is not always the case, however, and is just one of many considerations of which recording engineers should be aware.

When looking at approaches to finding how musicians should set about recording in order to achieve the best or most desirable results that meet a given brief, there may be issues with spill when the artists initially perform together (see Glossary). Here we need to consider how spill may impact the recording as a whole, and how decisions made at the recording stage can affect those made during post-production. When applied to the use of microphones in recording, spill occurs when an unintended instrument or sound source is captured via a microphone intended to capture something else.

A typical example might be when we solo a recorded channel of an acoustic guitar and other sounds, such as drums or a vocal, can be heard on the channel. Such a mixture of sound can be viewed in many ways by the practitioner. The recorded sound with spill could, for example, be seen as being 'blended' together and the spill is effectively viewed as complementary when played in the context of the record with the other performers. It is all about the brief and context of what is being recorded.

By contrast, such spill could sometimes be seen as problematic when a practitioner wishes to craft or manipulate a recorded sound during post-production to enhance or even exaggerate the listening soundstage. The spill could, for example, impact the use of upward compression when the engineer may wish to create a hyped-up, larger than life sound by altering the shape and envelope of a given recorded sound.

Contrary to some misconceptions, spill is not always the enemy. Rather than trying to avoid it when recording certain styles of music and types of performance, as an engineer we should embrace it. Indeed, many practitioners set up additional microphones in order to ride into the spill and in turn give themselves more options when it comes to balancing and blending the overall sounds on the recording.

There are many hybrid approaches with a wide range of factors to be taken into consideration, and ultimately solutions can be found to any given situation, at least within reason, since recording in any shape or form is not a perfect discipline.

The main lesson to take from this section is that as a practitioner you are required to plan ahead and think about these approaches in advance of a session. Over time this becomes easier and, with some practice, weighing up what approach or combination of approaches to take becomes almost second nature.

One solution to achieving a recording with minimal or no spill at all, while still allowing musicians to play live together to capture that all important performance with feel, is to separate the musicians with acoustic baffle boards (partitions). You could also place the musicians and/or their amps, for example, in different rooms. This, however, is no easy feat if you do not have the space or budget to facilitate such a recording. Many of the small project and budget studios today are limited to a small live room and possibly a vocal booth.

GAIN AND TRIM (LEVEL)

Gain staging is an important consideration when approaching a recording (and when mixing), and some of the basic aspects to consider include 'signal to noise ratio' (SNR), tone shaping, unity gain and headroom.

Before we delve any deeper, it would be a good starting point to try to visualise the distinction between amplification and level in the context of tone shaping when it comes to recording.

Gain is often associated with amplification and tone shaping, whilst trim is related to level or, more specifically in this example, the level going to tape (the recording level being sent to your recording device and DAW).

Take the example of a given preamplifier well known for its tone and how the electronics within the preamp impact the sound being passed through it. Such preamplifiers can be visualised as altering the shape and colour (tone) of the original sound, so that when it comes out the other end the shape and colour have been altered and in some cases exaggerated.

Gain, measured in decibels, is at its most basic the process whereby a given circuit within a preamp, for example, amplifies a signal being fed through it. Amplification is the process of increasing the voltage, power or current of a signal. In the case of a microphone and preamplifier, we are using the gain staging to take very small changes in voltage and amplify them to a usable level. The usable level is often referred to as 'line level', though it is worth noting that there are different 'line levels' cited for both professional and consumer use.

In regards to recording, gain is also used to add tone to a signal. Sometimes this change in tone is referred to as adding 'colour'. The type of preamp chosen, and more specifically the electronics and circuitry used to amplify the signal, can yield very different results. Traditionally vacuum tubes (valves) were used, but now there are also integrated circuits and transistors. Sometimes a combination is used alongside various types of transformers, which themselves add distortion to colour a sound, improve issues with noise and make a contribution in terms of how smoothly a signal can be stepped up or down when it comes

Universal Audio Solo 110 preamplifier with separate 'gain' (left) and 'level' controls (right).

to amplifying a given signal. The differences in the resultant sound can be overwhelmingly noticeable. Some preamps sound like they are adding low frequency body and resonance: what could be compared to a small pea can come out the other end more akin to a golf ball. In audio terms, more distortion or harmonic resonance, often odd low frequency harmonics created via magnetic flux, can give the sound a larger full-bodied tone.

My analogy of a pea growing to the size of a golf ball is definitely exaggerated, but so is the change

to the signal being passed through certain types of preamp.

Preamps without transformers are renowned for how clean and transparent they sound, so it is not always about adding tone. Signal to noise ratio can be a very important factor in terms of being able to amplify low level signals by a significant amount in order to bring the signals up to a usable level, especially in very dynamic music such as classical or jazz, when the engineer needs to keep the inherent noise issues associated with electrical equipment attenuated.

When it comes to setting recording levels and gain staging, there is no 'one size fits all' target value. Whether you are measuring peaks or averages, it is mainly about a good signal to noise ratio, the dynamic range of the signal and headroom. When recording to a tape machine, overloading the signal can create symmetrical saturation, which, depending on the bias, can audibly add low frequency and odd harmonic distortion, among other spectral attributes. The result can be a pleasing addition. Digital clipping and distortion, however, should be avoided. A level of around −18dBFS is only a suggestion. Signals will fluctuate and you can aim for higher peak values. Just keep an eye on your meters and an ear on the sound.

Unfortunately at times some equipment in need of maintenance or not really suitable as a professional tool for a certain type of job can actually bring the noise floor up to unusable levels if the practitioner tries to push the gain too much. Signal to noise can also be considered in practical application terms as the ratio between the wanted signal and the unwanted signal, such as background noise. When conducting an interview on location, for example, the recordist may decide to place a microphone much closer to the wanted sound source, in this case the person being interviewed, rather than holding the microphone away at a distance, in order to avoid unwanted background noise, which can begin to equal or even mask (hide or obscure) the wanted signal.

When starting out many people would advise using metering to help applying gain in a manner that amplifies the incoming signal to a level that

A section from the modular, custom Neve A258 console at Le Mob studios in London. The preamps are well known for their distinctive tone and colour.

masks the background noise, but avoids distorting the sound, by pushing the electronics of the preamp. Most modern engineers will find themselves recording to a DAW using an interface or other digital device in which the original analogue signal or voltage needs to pass through converters, specifically the analogue to digital stage (A/D), where the amplitude of the varying incoming voltage is measured continuously and converted into binary code.

In this respect, when considering gain staging the recording engineer should be aware of decibels that are relative to full scale (dBFS). Unlike various analogue units of measurement such as volume units or 'VU', which can produce pleasing results near or around a measurement of 0dBVU, depending on calibration, you should avoid readings anywhere near 0dBFS as you run the risk of digitally clipping the signal. Unlike distortion in analogue systems, digital distortion is frowned upon for many reasons, not least for how harsh it sounds.

A good starting point in terms of headroom may be to look at levels of around −18dBFS, which equates to 0dBVU, although this depends whether you are looking at peak or averages (root mean square, RMS) when gain staging an incoming signal. It is far from a perfect science as incoming signals are dynamic, unlike the sine wave here shown for demonstration purposes.

This is where trim or selecting the level to tape, or your chosen recording device, comes into play. I would suggest that, after some practice, it is all about using your ears, breaking away from convention when being creative and trying to avoid digital clipping or any audible unwanted distortion or artefacts.

If you have amplified a signal with preamps that house particular transformers, or for example germanium transistors, and other elements used for controlling electric current, then depending on the job at hand it can be very pleasing to push this kind of circuitry in order to enhance the tones and colour, creating a larger than life sound if you like. In this scenario, once you have acquired the tone you may find that the level going to your recording device is too hot and digital clipping takes place.

This is where either a fader on a mixing console or a trim/level control on a preamp comes into play. Use your ears to achieve a sound and tone you are happy with and then use the trim to adjust the output level going to your recording device. You are not altering the amplification and tone of the incoming signal and sound you have crafted, but just the level at which that sound is to be recorded. In the case of my highly exaggerated analogy, you still have a golf ball but you can alter the level to make sure the recording device captures the golf ball in all its glory, leaving you headroom to balance the sound and add further processing during post-production, if needed, while avoiding digital clipping at the A/D stage of conversion.

Gain staging will also impact how various pieces of outboard equipment respond within a given signal chain and this can lead to all sorts of creative outcomes. On a mixing console the preamps will often be driven to alter how the EQ responds as many equalisation tools and devices emulate or use similar circuitry to that already touched upon, such as transformers. This can also be said of outboard equipment. An engineer will often use a combination of tone shaping and dynamic processing to create a larger than life sound. An obvious candidate would be upward compression, by which the envelope of the sound changes and tones that had previously decayed away can be brought up in the record. In practice many compressors will add tone as well as process the dynamics and shape of an incoming sound.

In summation, certain electronic components in hardware like preamplifiers or a plugin attempting to emulate the hardware can be driven to create additional tone. If they are then daisy chained to another piece of hardware within the signal chain, gain staging can impact how the additional equipment reacts. This can alter tone and so gain staging is a bit more of a consideration than simply attaining a suitable recording level and masking the noise floor inherent in electrical systems.

As always I would remind you that we are touching the surface here and recommend you look into concepts such as 'total harmonic distortion' (THD). Indeed, it can be said that any time a signal is passed through amplifiers, transducers such a microphone or any equipment used to direct, transmit or process a signal, then some form of distortion will manifest. When looking at distortion you should consider the transients, phase, dynamics, crossovers and non-linear variations of any signal being processed. There are also limitations to bandwidth and non-uniform responses when looking at how a signal is distorted after passing through circuitry in amplifiers, transducers and other tools used for signal processing.

SETTING LEVELS AND GAIN STAGING AS A PRACTICAL APPLICATION

Gain staging can be a very creative process with some consideration. Many electric guitarists work with gain for tone shaping and level from the outset, cranking the gain to get the all-important sound they desire, and then (hopefully) turning the level down so that the rest of the band in the rehearsal room do not disown them or go deaf.

From a practical point of view is it always good to opt for additional tone when recording, regardless of the level going to tape? The simple answer is no, though of course it depends on the job at hand. When recording a jazz trio or classical ensemble, for example, unless otherwise briefed the role of the recording engineer is more akin to that of a sonic photographer. Let me elaborate on this.

When taking a photograph we often just want to capture a moment in time. It could be to mark a special occasion, for example when one of my children blows a candle out on a birthday cake. When this photograph is being taken I am not trying to force the issue or present a hyper reality, I am just simply wanting to capture the moment so I can look back at a later date with fond memories. I have no doubt that I could pass the photo in question to an expert who could then work some magic in order to enhance it in a number of ways, but keeping the photo simple and natural is very different to choreographing it in an attempt to craft a picture to suit a particular narrative.

The same goes for recording. Sometimes it's not about pushing the gain staging for tone enhancement or using fancy signal chains. If we are trying to capture a natural performance then it is about finding a good sounding space to record in, choosing appropriate microphones and their effective placement, and applying suitable techniques. Here, in the most basic manner, gain staging or 'setting levels' is more about masking the noise floor and leaving plenty of headroom for a dynamic performance, avoiding clipping.

Often in these scenarios it is good to use the same type of preamp for an element of continuity and many practitioners like to use more transparent amplifiers without transformers. You may also find that setting levels to similar values is a more subtle approach than full-on manipulation and sound reinforcement. I would advise starting out by amplifying all the signals by the same amount and then sitting back and listening. Give the musicians the headroom and space (not in the acoustic sense) to perform, rather than you pushing the levels and gain staging to effectively alter the balance of the intended performance.

Again, there is no 'one size fits all' approach when it comes to gain staging and a good place to start would be to get familiar with various types of metering, which provide a visual guide while simultaneously training your ears. With the latter it helps to push signals within various signal paths from analogue through to digital in order to hear how distortion can audibly manifest.

I would highly recommend undertaking further reading and getting used to the concept of 'unity gain'. A very succinct explanation of this process is that the output of a signal should be equal to the signal level at the input stage. In essence what is fed into a given piece of equipment, or more specifically is passed through the equipment's electrical components, is what comes out in terms of level.

This becomes more complex as further equipment is inserted into a signal chain for either creative or corrective practice, and when calibration is taken into consideration.

Ultimately, though, unity gain allows an engineer to create a sense of parity and provides much needed headroom, whether a signal is processed or unprocessed, when the various pieces of equipment in the signal chain are bypassed.

In a more contemporary fashion, try to think of unity gain at the mixing stage and while working 'in the box' with your chosen DAW. Though I am not going to talk in terms of passing 1 volt through a given piece of equipment and getting 1 volt out, regardless of whether the equipment is active or in a state of bypass, think of what happens when you insert a plugin (spectral, dynamic or otherwise) onto a channel in your DAW. Regardless of what the plugin does to the sound you are feeding through it, here the level should be the same going in as it is going out. Here you can perform an 'AB' test between the clean (bypassed) signal and the processed (plugin activated) signal. Using appropriate metering that measures averages, peaks or a combination of these, as well as your ears, you are looking to achieve parity between the input and output signal, regardless of the state of the plugin or hardware. This allows for more headroom and the additional use of processors, if so required.

In terms of mixing and balancing our various sounds at the recording stage or during post-production we can then move a fader up to bring the processed or unprocessed sounds to the forefront of a mix or bring the fader down to lower them. There is more to take into consideration, however, when it comes to the specific size, spread and placement of the sound on a given channel within the mix and listening soundstage.

When unity gain is not considered, the summing together of the various signals occupying your multitrack channels will quickly reduce any headroom within a mix and this can be seen clearly when viewing the meters on the master fader.

When recording an engineer should take unity gain into consideration in terms of signal to noise ratios, noise floors and clipping. However, depending on the type of recording, equipment being used, calibration and what a practitioner wishes to achieve in terms of tone shaping, signals may be pushed and balance can be revised at a later date. Again, there is 'no one size fits all', but I would suggest it is prudent for any budding engineer to be mindful of such concepts.

In terms of unity gain and gain staging, notable pieces of hardware intended for such purposes as amplification, tone shaping or dynamic processing, as well as the emulations based on them, can be underfed as well as overly driven at the output stage.

GAIN STAGING, SETTING LEVELS AND PANNING WHEN RECORDING IN STEREO

When it comes to recording in stereo many engineers have access to purpose-built stereo microphones. There are also microphones that work with the principle of ambisonics and can record sound sources three-dimensionally from a given source point. The sound source captured in this way can be phase coherently folded down for stereophonic reproduction purposes. Such specialist microphones come with their own unique XLR cable, which can have five or more female pins and break into two or four male pin XLR cables.

Alongside this many practitioners may invest in specialist preamps that provide gain to all the channels equally and simultaneously.

This may not be an option for many engineers, however, and therefore stereo recording techniques or arrays used for multichannel surround or higher-order channel-based reproduction systems often employ multiple single, mono microphones.

We will be looking at this in more detail in Chapter 5, but for now it is worth mentioning that when you are overseeing the process of gain staging and sending the levels to tape, or your chosen DAW, for the purpose of recording in stereo you should try to match the settings of your various controls, be that the gain, trim, faders, or whatever else you may be using to send a given signal to your chosen recording medium.

If your first microphone has been set to +40dB, then the second microphone in the stereo configuration should be amplified by +40dB, the trim or output level on your preamp or fader on your mixing console should also be at the same level value on both channels.

This will all make more sense after you have read Chapter 5, but for now just be aware that mismatched levels in terms of the gain structure and subsequent output recording levels will impact the stereophonic image you are trying to capture of a given sound source within the space you have chosen to record.

During post-production you can cause a sound image to shift when altering the levels of faders, and this is why many practitioners prefer to use two mono audio channels in their chosen DAW rather than one stereo channel.

Another aspect to consider is how you pan your channels. With a stereo audio channel this will normally be done for you, but if you opt to use two separate mono channels directly into your DAW or via a mixing console, you will need to hard-pan one channel to the left and the other to the right, otherwise you will not get the time and level differences from the speakers or headphones at the reproduction stage, resulting in two mono sounds of equal gain within both speakers or headphones. Again, we will look at this in more detail in subsequent chapters.

Another consideration when recording In stereo and applying panning is to decide from what perspective the listener will be listening. Let us go back to the idea of a recording being like a canvas, with microphones creating an audible picture of sound just as paintbrushes, crayons and other tools define shapes, size and colour. Is the listener in the picture looking out at those in the gallery or are they in the gallery staring into the picture?

Making such decisions early on in a recording helps with cohesion and continuity on many levels, not least when additional spot microphones are added to focus on and record a specific instrument or instruments within a soundstage being captured by a stereo configuration or larger array of microphones. For more detail on this *see* Chapter 7.

3
MICROPHONE TECHNIQUES FOR RECORDING

At the risk of repeating myself, microphones can be placed close to a source, at a distance or anywhere in-between. You will hear such terms as 'accent', 'spot', 'direct', 'distant', 'room' and 'ambient' being applied when it comes to explaining how microphones are placed in relation to a given sound source. If we place a microphone close to a sound source then we can expect to capture more of the source in question with less of the room sound.

By contrast, if a microphone is placed further away from a sound source then you will capture more of the room sound. This can be a really effective way to add depth and indeed width, the latter by applying stereo techniques, to the listening soundstage. Such techniques can be used in a creative manner within an interesting sounding space, controlled (acoustically treated) or otherwise. However, there are occasions when considerations such as standing waves (related nodes and antinodes), and an unflattering reverberation time and characteristic can yield unusable results.

There is also the concept to consider that the closer a microphone is placed to a given sound source, the less natural it sounds. This particularly applies to acoustic instruments and the voice. This is in part due to the idea of restricted sound propagation in relation to how an instrument resonates. From where does the sound we hear emanate?

The basic idea is that by providing more space between the instrument and the microphones we can capture a more holistic and natural tone, albeit often far from how we actually hear sound in terms of realism, instead of immersing oneself in the sound, which requires a whole other set of

factors to be considered. Remember microphones resemble drawing tools or paintbrushes in many ways: it is how they are configured that makes the difference. Placing a very sensitive microphone too close to a sound source can capture all sorts of unwanted distortions, but can also be useful in making an instrument sound larger than life and exaggerated, while capturing less room spill, and the resulting sound may have its place within the production process.

If the microphone is positioned further away, then acoustics and the sound of the room will play a part in impacting the quality of the recording. Often engineers work with a compromise somewhere in-between in terms of microphone placement. Since for many practitioners it is all about options, when it comes to recording, engineers will often use a combination of multiple microphones placed close, at a distance and anywhere in-between. What is captured can then be used in a variety of ways to paint a picture of sound for the listener.

When I started out as a recording engineer I had a habit of using as many microphones as I could get my hands on, but nowadays I often use fewer. Looking back, I would not necessarily say that the practice was wrong. There is certainly a lot to gain from experimenting through using the best tool of all, your ears. Indeed, using a variety of microphones always provides options at various stages of the record production process.

Choice is arguably a good thing. Capturing various instruments and sounds with multiple microphone types from different positions or vantage points allows for more control in post-production, often enabling a varied perspective in more than one sense.

I have just found myself using fewer microphones as I have become more adept over time, developing a better understanding of the many other factors that impact a recording session, such as room acoustics, tuning and performance technique.

The truth is that with a bit of knowledge, consideration of associated theory and plenty of practice you can achieve some interesting results, especially if you train your ears over time by listening to reference tracks and learning the practical relevance and application of a few basic measurement tools.

INVERTING POLARITY

Phase/time alignment, phase shifts, image distortion, destructive interference and so on are all concepts we will look at in far more detail during the final chapter.

As a rule of thumb, however, when you are using multiple microphones to record a sound source you should consider the polarity of the incoming signal.

Microphones work as transducers and changes in SPL are represented as changes in voltage, which go through a positive and negative phase in a given cycle. If a sound source is captured via multiple microphones, there is always a possibility that the signals being captured are out of polarity from one another. This can be as simple as something like a microphone cable being wired incorrectly or different phase shifts resulting from the distances between the microphones. This is another subject we will look at in more detail later.

When you are using multiple microphones, especially if they are facing one another, and so pointing in opposite directions, make sure you take the time to experiment with flipping the polarity on one (or more) of the channels on your mixing console or preamplifier. Most audio interfaces will also provide this option.

3:1 RULE

Not all practitioners agree on this principle, at least in terms of its practical application. But I would posit it is good for beginners to be mindful of the concept and experiment listening in mono (if necessary) when setting up multiple microphones. There are some misconceptions when it comes to discussing the rule in relation to the theory of phase coherence and the manifestation of destructive interference. Such interference can occur, mostly but not exclusively, when multiple microphones in close proximity are used simultaneously to capture differing sources such as an ensemble, and these sources are then summed into mono. The basic idea is that when recording with multiple microphones, you will achieve better results if the second microphone is positioned at least three times (or more) the distance as that between the first microphone and the sound source(s). For example, If you place a microphone 60cm away from a vocalist, the second microphone being used to capture the second vocalist should be at least 180cm away from the first microphone and vice versa (Note that this does not apply when considering stereo configurations).

When microphones are moved further away from one another in relation to the given source they are intending to capture there is an attenuation in level in terms of what the microphones capture. You can think about a sort of ratio between the wanted sound source in front of a given microphone and the unwanted (spill) from another sound source. Although this may make for a more pleasing sound when summed, there is more to consider when it comes to minimising issues pertaining to the phase relationships of summed signals and phase coherence.

MONO vs STEREO

Whether talking about recording or playing back audio, I have often found many people are confused by the difference between monophonic

The red light recording sign at Le Mob studios instructing people not to walk into the live room while recording is taking place.

(mono for short) and stereophonic (stereo) sound. The latter can be even more confusing when sound localisation is discussed.

Perhaps a good place to start is by discussing how sound is delivered by playback systems. Using loudspeakers as part of the example, mono recordings and mixes for playback will play the exact same sound sources, or more specifically the balance of the sound sources, through a single speaker to any number of speakers you may wish to utilise. In essence the same mix is played in every speaker whether it's one or one hundred. The overall sound picture created by the engineer can be projected and created by one speaker if necessary.

Stereo playback on the other hand is when sound sources can be positioned and played back discretely in separate speakers. In basic stereophonic playback systems you have a separate left and right channel to place sound and playback within a discrete left and right speaker. The overall sound picture and listening experience is on this occasion being created by the two separate speakers.

As with mono, stereophonic playback can be played through many speakers, although normally some type of matrixing is required in order to preserve the discrete information originally placed in either the left or right channel.

Multichannel playback systems employ more than two discrete channels. The most basic is three channels, providing the engineer with a separate

left, centre and right channel to work with. After this point we can add channels, or specifically in this example speakers, in order to envelop the listener and provide the engineer with the option of recording and mixing with a 360-degree sound-stage in mind.

A basic quadrophonic system adds a left and right rear speaker to a standard left and right front-facing stereo listening soundstage to reproduce a 360-degree listening soundstage. A 5.1 surround sound system employs the front three channel speakers (left, centre and right), with additional speakers, sometimes referred to as satellites, placed behind the listener as left surround (LS) and right surround (RS). The '.1' refers to the LFE (low frequency enhancement or subwoofer), which does not provide a full frequency response within the audible range.

Further speakers can be placed above the listener to introduce three-dimensional sound that includes height cues (periphony). Dolby Atmos and Aura 3D are two systems that offer channel-based solutions of this type.

The difference between mono, stereo and multi-channel systems can be simplified by citing the options the user is given by being able to place different sources into discrete channels and speakers. Of course great records have been recorded and mixed in mono and an engineer can still balance sources and attain some sense of depth.

Stereophonic sound is preferable to mono in many ways, for example the listener can gain a sense of width as well as depth, making it easier to place where a sound source is coming from. This premise continues as we use additional speakers to envelop the listener. Stereo and multichannel playback systems that use discrete channels and speakers are nominally considered two-dimemsional, because sound is projected on the horizontal plane. When additional channels are added and sent to discrete speakers that are placed above the listener, then technically we are now projecting sound with height cues from the vertical plane, making this a three-dimensional delivery system.

This a much simplified and stripped-down explanation and I have left out many specialist considerations associated with this field of study. But trust me, it will all help when we move into discussing recording techniques.

At this point I would suggest that a good stereo recording and mix played over, for example, two speakers can conjure up phantom images and create an illusionary sense of three dimensions for the listener. Here, width is associated with where a sound source emanates from left to right between the speakers (or outside of the speakers), depth, between the front and back of the listening soundstage, and in line with frequency projection, psychoacoustic considerations, spatial dynamics and a combination of other factors, a practitioner can consider where a sound source appears to be emanating in terms of a top to bottom axis, if you consider the listening soundstage to take the shape of an imaginary cube.

One of the 'other factors' relates directly to how we hear sound and measure sound at the ears. I would recommend looking at head-related transfer functions (HRTFs), as again I am only offering a simple and concise explanation.

If you now compare the opposite of a speaker, which is technically a microphone (in terms of being a transducer), in relation to what we have discussed in terms of speakers it becomes apparent why recording engineers use a combination of mono and stereo techniques, and sometimes multiple microphones in a specialised array, in order to paint a picture of sound. Where a speaker or speakers are used to recreate an overall picture or 'image' of sound at the playback stage for the listener, a recording engineer uses microphones to capture an image or picture in the first instance, hence the earlier metaphor in Chapter 1 of a microphone resembling a drawing tool or paintbrush.

In part a recording engineer often wants to capture a sense of depth, width and localisation – there may also be very specialist recordings when the engineer wants to capture a sense of height – of a given sound source within the listening soundstage to create that overall image and picture for the listener. Let's take a look at some techniques.

Multiple mono microphone technique: A Brauner Phantom V (upper left), a Bock 195 (upper right) and a Coles 4038 (underneath the piano) are being used to capture various tones emanating from the piano.

In the example illustrated here, three microphones are being used simply to capture some of the many different tones that resonate and emanate from a piano. Each microphone has a different transient response, frequency response, polar response pattern and sensitivity. With a bit of practice these differences can be used in a complementary and sometimes flattering manner to capture the different sounds coming from the instrument.

In this instance we could then just balance the various sounds, checking the polarity, and if we choose place the various sounds via a panner (pan pot) on a mixer into either the left or right speaker. This would be making use of the stereo sound field or listening soundstage in terms of where each of the different sounds is placed, but it is not stereographic or, more specifically, it does not present the user with near controlled or correlated localisation cues. I will explain later, but for now I just want to highlight another example where multiple microphones may be used to capture various tones. In this instance I would most likely not use any panning and would opt solely for balancing the various sounds via faders. There are many situations when this approach is effective, but for this example I will use the double bass.

Place one microphone a metre or so from the body of the instrument, to capture more of the lower frequencies and resonance, and another higher up, slightly closer to the neck of the instrument to capture more of the performance articulation and additional tone to better capture a spectral balance.

In this example you can experiment with using different microphones, but a good starting point is to have a microphone with a good bass frequency response and an omni-polar response pattern to coincide with the nature of how low-frequency sound propagates as less directional wave energy. Conversely, when selecting a microphone to place nearer to the neck of the instrument, you could play around with using a directional polar response pattern that focuses more on the directional ray energy of mid-range and higher frequencies. It is

again an example of using your ears and deciding what you like.

Another benefit of using multiple microphones – and a tip during post-production – is that by altering just the balance of, in this case, the microphone used to capture the body of the instrument (placed lower down facing the bridge on- or off-centre), you can introduce space for other timbres and sounds within the listening soundstage, since retaining the other microphone placed higher up and facing the neck still provides much of the detail to allow the instrument to cut through the mix.

Again there is much more to consider when using multiple microphones on a given sound source, such as phase coherence, which we will be looking at in Chapter 8. Many recording engineers pay attention to issues pertaining to phase coherence, namely destructive interference and image distortion, when approaching a recording and such technical considerations will inform microphone placement. Working with my students over many years, however, I have found that often practitioners gain a better understanding of phase coherence during post-production. This in turn leads them to knowing what to listen out in the future for during the recording process and therefore leads to better practice when setting up and placing microphones. Practise, practise and practise some more.

Let us now return to stereophonic recording and the idea of localisation cues. It is arguably in part a question of correlation, with two or more microphones positioned so that the information they capture can be compared in order to decipher where a sound is emanating from within a given space.

If microphones are placed independently of one another with no specific relationship in terms of controlled and thought-out placement, specifically in regards to the angles and/or distance between the microphones, then the chances are they are unrelated and therefore not part of a stereo technique or more considered microphone array.

Stereo microphone techniques (like the example shown in the illustration on page 42) can be considered on a basic level to work in a similar manner to how we localise sound with our ears, which in part localise sound based on interaural level differences (ILDs) and interaural time differences (ITDs). There are also interaural intensity differences based on spectral content amongst other factors.

In the case of stereo microphones or when creating a stereo recording by placing more than one microphone together in a specific manner, we are allowing the microphones to capture time differences, level and intensity differences, or by using a combination of all of these.

CRITICAL DISTANCE

Whether you choose to use one microphone or many, as part of an array or just as a paint brush to capture different tones and colour from a given sound source(s), the placement of the microphones has a major impact on the recording.

A microphone can be placed close to a given sound source (direct placement), at a distance (ambient), or anywhere in between. The ratio between the direct sound and the reverberant sound (ambient sound based on the room's acoustics), however, will alter depending on the distance from the sound source being recorded.

The size, geometry and surface materials within the space you are recording in will play a part, as the reverberation characteristic and RT60 of the environment impacts the recorded sound.

Critical distance, like many of the theoretical considerations cited in this book, can be examined in far more detail. When just starting out on your journey as a recording engineer, however, just visualise the point where direct sound and reverberant sound are at equal levels (SPLs) within a given environment. This phenomenon is an important consideration when setting up a listening environment

and experience created via loudspeakers. When recording it impacts the choice of where to place your microphones.

In simple practical terms as a new recording engineer, critical distance can be seen as the crossing point at which the reverberant sound you are working with audibly takes over from the direct sound, at least in terms of what your microphones are capturing. It is the point at which the ratio between the direct and reverberant sound is no longer equal or comparable.

A good example in terms of where the audible effects of passing the point of critical distance can be heard is often exhibited in a larger space where a noticeable reverberation characteristic is evident. If you find yourself recording in a space with a noticeable RT60 time, it can be hard to make out consonants in speech at points of the room where the reverberant sound is higher in SPL than the direct sound.

When the recording loses definition, clarity or intelligibility, the recordist may consider moving the microphone. Although critical distance may be more of a consideration in a larger space, a recording engineer can often benefit greatly from making adjustments to placement of the microphone before reaching for any heavy-handed spectral processing.

It goes without saying that many practitioners deliberately work with setting up microphones to capture more of the reverberant sound for creative purposes.

STEREO RECORDING ANGLES (SRAs)

Michael Williams and others working in the field of sound recording are truly inspirational, especially when it comes to grasping the principles associated with stereo recording. I highly recommend his *Microphone Arrays for Stereo and Multichannel Sound Recording*, volumes 1 and 2, as well as many other papers published in various journals.

Williams has been credited with the conception of a stereo recording angle (SRA). The simplest explanation of an SRA is that it is the recording coverage or area that a stereo microphone configuration is capable of capturing. In effect it is the virtual image created for the listener over two speakers during playback.

Again I am only presenting a very watered down version of the concept and there are many other factors a practitioner should examine in order to truly understand the theoretical considerations associated with SRAs when intending to record a soundstage.

Nevertheless, it is good to try to visualise the concept, and with further research and subsequent practice I have no doubt that the quality of your recordings will improve. Let's imagine a *Mission Impossible* type of scenario where the agents must gain access to a well-guarded piece of high-tech equipment and invisible laser sensors are being used for security. Often in the movies we see sensors and potential barriers to the prize being overcome by using some sort of spray to reveal where the said laser sensors begin and end. The invisible becomes visible to the naked eye.

SRAs are very similar in some respects as we cannot see them when recording. When we listen back to a recording, however, all is revealed. In essence a SRA is the area, or more specifically the sector, being captured by the combined microphones being used, and subsequently the virtual image created via speakers for the listener. SRAs are inversely proportional to the set-up angle between the microphones: if the angle is 90 degrees, for example, then the SRA is wider than microphones angled at 110 degrees.

In most cases, however, one could argue that the most pressing aspect of any recording is how it sounds to the end user, to the listener.

Different SRAs will in essence determine whether a sound source or sources are located within the virtual image played back via speakers. Are the given sounds emanating in a more central position between the speakers, further out towards the extremities of the left and right speakers or nicely spread across the whole listening soundstage?

Considering the idea of the listening soundstage at this juncture is again not a bad idea when different SRAs can impact on the virtual size, localisation and definition of a given sound source or multiple sources, as well as impact the ratio between direct and reverberant sound.

As a recording engineer, if you start thinking about the listening soundstage from the outset in terms of how big a sound may be perceived and where a given sound is located from left to right and front to back (depth), then learning about SRAs and experimenting with various stereo recording techniques will help you improve your skills. It will also, from a creative perspective, arguably help you to plan ahead in terms of crafting your production and deciding where to place various sounds within the perceived listening soundstage.

It is worth noting that in many instances when SRAs are being discussed the recording engineer is often choosing a suitable stereo technique to capture a soundstage inhabited by a musical ensemble. When recording on location it is the engineer's job to consider the SRA in order to capture the live performance, often in a way that attempts to capture a realistic and natural-sounding recording.

Part of this consideration would entail the recordist being aware of the concept of 'angular distortion'. Michael Williams suggests that 'geometric' or 'angular' distortions are the variations of where various sound sources are placed within the virtual soundstage (at the reproduction stage), and such distortions alter depending on the SRA you have chosen to work with. Put simply, such distortions could create a virtual image in which certain instruments within the ensemble or orchestra being recorded are effectively pushed towards the extremities of the virtual soundstage. This could be visualised as the various sounds being bunched up and overlapping one another, either between the speakers or to the outer reaches of the image created via the left and right speaker. By contrast, if you choose a more appropriate stereo technique

AB30 spaced pair: time of arrival stereo configured with two AKG C414 microphones set to omnipolar response patterns.

and placement so that the SRA captured suits the soundstage you are recording, then you will minimise angular distortion and, in theory, the various sounds within the ensemble or orchestra should be more evenly distributed and placed over the virtual image or listening soundstage.

Nevertheless, one can always argue that the brief you are working with will dictate the choices you make. Not all recordings require you to capture a soundstage in which the various sounds to be played back are spread evenly over the virtual image. As my students often suggest, if it sounds good, it is good. Liking how something sounds is, after all, ultimately subjective.

Your job, in part, as a practitioner is to utilise knowledge, explore theoretical concepts, practise and gain experience in order to navigate any issue or potential problem that may arise during a recording session.

Given that, many recording engineers use multiple stereo techniques that each yield different SRAs in order to capture and localise various sounds within the listening soundstage. Using varied techniques, either simultaneously as part of a live recording or while overdubbing, can widen the range of options and perspectives when manipulating the listening soundstage. This in turn will impact the overall listening experience.

TIME OF ARRIVAL STEREO

Microphones arranged in a time of arrival stereo configuration have a clear and defined distance

AB60 spaced pair: time of arrival stereo configured with two AKG C414 microphones set to omnipolar response patterns.

between them. The technique illustrated here is often referred to as an 'AB spaced pair'. Since the placement between the microphones, or more specifically the distance between the diaphragms of the two microphones, in this case is 30cm, the technique is often called AB30 for short.

When we talk about sound localisation we are, in the simplest of explanations, referring to the process by which we determine from which direction a sound is emanating. In the practical sense of how a recording engineer uses this information, we are more concerned with how the end user or listener can pinpoint and place where a given sound source is located within the listening soundstage.

Time of arrival stereo techniques such as AB30 provide localisation cues of a sound source or sources being recorded based upon the time differences of a given sound source arriving and being captured by the two microphones being utilised.

When the engineer places the separate signals captured via the two microphones into their own discrete channel, by panning one microphone hard left and one hard right, we can provide the listener with the same time differences originally measured and in essence compared between the two diaphragms.

Recording with time of arrival stereo will always localise the sound source as coming from an area of the listening soundstage closest to the microphone used in the stereo technique chosen or array at the time of recording. Conversely, once the recorded signals have been panned, when we listen back the same sound source will play back

XY90 coincident: intensity stereo configured with two AKG C451 B microphones with cardioid polar response patterns, shown in the same configuration but displayed from different angles.

from a given speaker with time differences from the other speaker(s) and in turn arrive at our ears at different times. These ITDs help us to pinpoint roughly where the sound is coming from. I say 'roughly' because time of arrival stereo and spaced arrays in general are not hugely accurate beyond a certain distance in terms of point source recording and localisation. They do, however, provide a more expansive listening area in terms of the size and can sound more enveloping.

It is worth noting that with stereo techniques, or specifically when recording stereographic information with time of arrival differences to assist us in localising a sound during playback or reproduction via speakers, that we are dealing with a ratio between the most direct sound path, in this instance in terms of time, and variations of the various time differences that accumulate to present an image of a sound as well as from where it is emanating. We do not just get an impression that a given sound source is mainly coming from one speaker, but rather a balance between the two, a ratio between the closest distance and the furthest.

Unprocessed time of arrival stereo techniques are not generally mono compatible when a mix is folded down or 'downmixed' as phase coherence is compromised, and the summed signal suffers

XY110 coincident: intensity stereo configured with two AKG C451 B microphones with cardioid polar response patterns, shown in the same configuration but displayed from different angles.

via destructive interference, something we will look at in more detail in Chapter 8.

When setting up a spaced pair, such as AB30, it is preferable to use omnidirectional polar response patterns. This assists with comparative time differences as there are no off-axis attenuations in terms of the microphones' input-output sensitivity. In practice an omnidirectional polar response pattern also yields a flatter frequency response.

POPULAR TIME OF ARRIVAL STEREO TECHNIQUES (SPACED PAIR/ARRAYS):

AB30, AB60 and AB120

This technique generally uses two condenser microphones set to an omnipolar response pattern with the microphone diaphragms placed 30cm, 60cm or 120cm apart. Experiment with different polar response patterns and microphones, and as always use your ears to make your own judgement on how suitable the results are in relation to whatever project you may be working on.

Decca Tree

Sometimes referred to as ABC or LCR stereo, this technique utilises three microphones, usually condensers with omnidirectional polar response patterns, though patterns such as cardioid have also been used. The left and right microphones (LR) are spaced 2m apart and the signals captured are panned left and right. The third microphone is placed in the centre (C) and positioned 1.5m in front of the LR microphones, forming an isosceles triangle or the letter 'T' inverted. The LR microphones are placed at the rear of the array and the centre microphone is positioned to face the centre of the soundstage you are recording.

Using this technique is beneficial when you want to capture a larger performance area, though it would be considered over the top in a small live room or the average bedroom. When the spacings between microphones pass a certain point the correlation or relationship between the two microphones becomes irrelevant and the microphones can be seen as just independent microphones capturing sound transmission in a singular, monophonic fashion.

This is not quite the case with the spacing between the LR microphones in a Decca Tree, although adding a third microphone and positioning it 1m forward from the centre of the LR microphones in the array helps to provide a distinct centre image at the reproduction stage.

Arguably the Decca tree can also be down mixed to mono if just the centre microphone is used and the LR wide microphones are muted.

INTENSITY/LEVEL DIFFERENCE STEREO (COINCIDENT)

In the most basic of terms think of level differences as how loud a given signal or signals are, in this case when the variations or differences in levels are captured at the microphone's diaphragm(s).

Remember, though, that from a human hearing perspective perceived sound levels and SPLs are in no way equal and this varies at different frequencies. A microphone, however, is technically a mechanical device at least in terms of the diaphragm or ribbon playing its role.

Though level differences play a part in the localisation of a given sound source when using a time of arrival spaced stereo technique or multichannel array, there is no requirement to use a directional polar pattern.

In contrast, intensity or level difference stereo requires the microphone diaphragms to be as close to one another as possible in space and time without touching, in order to reduce the risk of mechanical noise, and the use of directional polar response patterns is paramount. (Note, however, that the MS technique can use a non-directional omni for the MID/SUM.)

Unlike time of arrival stereo, there are far fewer issues when folding down or 'down mixing' to mono as source point coincident recording is far more phase coherent, although some cancellation

Blumlein stereo recording technique using two AKG C414 condenser microphones, each set to a figure of 8 polar response pattern and placed at an angle of 90 degrees coincident to one another. To align the technique so that it is facing the centre of the soundstage, in this instance a guitar, treat the configuration in the same manner as when placing the XY90 technique. The centre of the SRA is considered to be where the microphone capsules become coincident or, if you prefer, meet up.

allow localisation cues to be captured based on level and intensity differences.

In Chapter 1 we looked at the point at which a directional microphone is most sensitive towards a given sound source, or more specifically an oncoming pressure wave. This position of the microphone is referred to as being 'on axis'. By placing two microphones coincidentally to one another we create a coverage area or stereo recording angle. When a practitioner uses any number of microphones using the intensity stereo

Two AKG C414 large diaphragm condensers arranged for the MS level difference/intensity stereo technique. The technique is normally configured using a centre (mid) microphone with a cardioid polar response pattern, here placed at the top of the configuration, facing the sound source you wish to capture or the centre point of a recording soundstage. Another microphone, preferably of a similar type and model, is placed at an angle of 90 degrees from the mid/centre microphone to work as a side channel. The microphone used to capture the side image is set to a bidirectional, figure of eight polar response pattern.

can still manifest. In essence the changing SPLs captured by the microphones placed in a given intensity stereo technique are occurring at near similar times when the ribbon or diaphragm is doing its job acting as a transducer.

This is not to say that off-axis colouration of the overall signal does not occur, or that the signal is 100 per cent phase coherent in finite detail when folded down to mono.

In the XY90 configuration the two condenser microphone diaphragms are placed as close to one another as possible and angled at 90 degrees. The two pencil condenser microphones in this instance have a cardioid polar response pattern and it is these directional patterns that

MS level difference/intensity stereo configuration using two different models of large diaphragm capacitor microphones, a Brauner Phantom V set to a figure of eight polar response pattern and an Avantone CK6.

using a cardioid polar response pattern. The virtual image created over speakers is contained within that coverage area and plays back in a more localised manner between the left and right speaker, with a more distinct phantom image in the centre of the virtual stereophonic image or listening soundstage.

Conversely, using a time of arrival stereo technique such as AB120 produces a much smaller SRA of around 50.8 degrees, and yet when you listen back to the virtual image created over speakers the recording sounds wider.

Once again, I would recommend further reading and the books and articles by Michael Williams and others would be an excellent place to point you in the right direction, even though Williams himself suggests you learn through doing and not by reading a book.

POPULAR INTENSITY/LEVEL DIFFERENCE STEREO (COINCIDENT) TECHNIQUES

XY90, XY110, XY120 and XY180

Normally formed of two condenser microphones, often pencil condensers, the capsules are placed as close together as possible and then angled at 90 degrees in the example of XY90.

Experiment with the various angles using a protractor. The microphones, except at 180 degrees, form a tip like an arrow that can be pointed at the centre of the sound source or soundstage. If you want to try the XY180 technique, then just use the centre point where the two capsules meet. The main thing is to listen and see how the off-axis attenuation in intensity levels impacts the image as a whole.

Ideally listen back via well-placed speakers as you train your ears to listen out for what constitutes a phantom image. Interaural Crosstalk plays a part here when listening via speakers. Spaced microphone configurations and the third set of stereo techniques we will be talking about in the next section will of course impact such images and yield different results. However, this is also true if you listen over headphones where crosstalk is not an issue. Put simply, different techniques sound

technique the SRA depends on the angles and polar response patterns used.

Smaller SRAs produce wider virtual images over the speakers and some intensity stereo techniques have large SRAs.

In the XY90 technique there is as near as possible to zero distance between the microphone capsules where the diaphragms are housed. These diaphragms are angled at 90 degrees from one another facing the soundstage. The XY90 technique yields an SRA of 195 degrees when different over various playback mediums, and some stereo techniques can sound less effective over headphones in terms of creating an illusionary image. Therefore, moving forward, it is worth reading about both acoustics and psychoacoustics, even the basics, in order to really understand why such mediums present both pros and cons when used to reproduce a listening experience.

When choosing your microphones, experiment with different polar response patterns such as hyper-cardioid, super-cardioid and sub-cardioid. The last of these is a wide cardioid that starts to yield less of a directional response in terms of sensitivity and is arguably closer to an omnipolar pattern in some instances, so you attain less of an image by way of capturing smaller variations in level between the microphones.

Blumlein Technique

Configured with two figure of eight polar response patterns, the technique named after Alan Blumlein, an EMI engineer who is credited by some as inventing stereo recording in the 1930s, uses either one stereo microphone with two separate ribbons or diaphragms or two microphones placed as close as possible to one another on a vertical axis, with the ribbons or diaphragms angled at 90 degrees from one another. Usually employing two ribbon microphones or, alternatively, variable condenser microphones, this coincident, intensity stereo technique uses two figure of eight polar patterns to capture an SRA of around 75.7 degrees.

The virtual stereo image this yields is comparatively wider between the speakers and within the listening soundstage than a XY90, for example, but it retains a decent phantom image. As with other intensity stereo techniques, localisation of sound sources is far more accurate in pinpointing their relative position than a more widely spaced time of arrival stereo technique, or 'spaced pair'.

MID SIDE (MS) STEREO

Sometimes referred to as 'sum and difference', the MS stereo technique, also credited as being

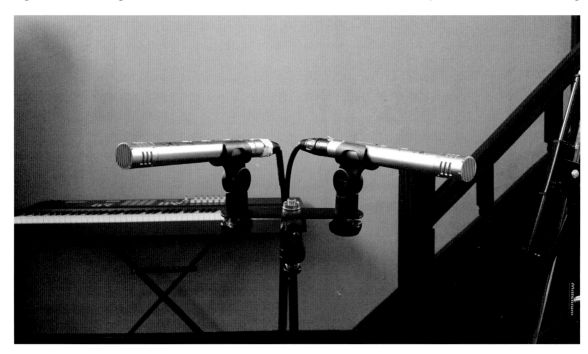

NOS equivalence stereo (mixed stereo) using two AKG C451 B pencil condensers with cardioid polar response patterns. There is a 30cm spacing between the microphone capsules, which are angled at 90 degrees away from one another.

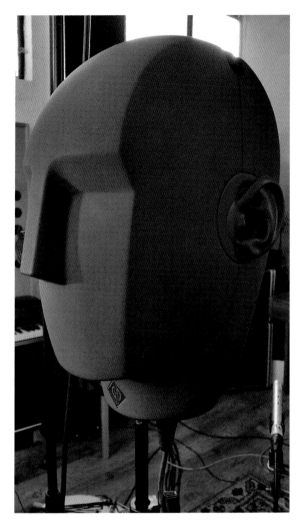

Neumann KU 100 binaural dummy head

and the side channels being panned hard left and fully right, respectively. MS is considered the best option for when mono compatibility is required because the LR signal is completely cancelled out when the stereo information is downmixed to mono, and only the centre channel remains, the Mid (sum) channel recorded via the microphone with a cardioid polar response pattern that typically faces the centre of the recorded soundstage.

There are ways of decoding the difference/side channels at the recording stage, but many practitioners choose to process the signal during post-production.

At the recording stage, for example, the engineer might parallel the signal captured by a microphone with a bi-directional pattern, normally via a patch bay, and return the signal to an additional channel on a mixing console. The polarity is then inverted on one of the two side channels and one panned hard left and the other fully to the right. This matrixed signal now gives the user a separate width channel (LR) and a centre channel (C).

Many practitioners will decode the side channel, which becomes the 'difference', during post-production either through some sort of matrix decoder plugin or by simply duplicating the side channel, then panning one fully to the left and one fully to the right, and inverting the polarity 180 degrees on one of the channels.

MS can offer some flexibility in terms of the set-up and what equipment you have at hand, because unlike other stereo techniques you can attain good results by using two different types of microphone. More specifically the two microphones do not need to be matched in terms of manufacturer, model and operating principle. Though technically a true matched pair of microphones in terms of frequency response and other specifications does not exist, it is highly recommended to try to use two of the same microphones for continuity. More specifically, two microphones of the exact same model will help to capture a more consistent image or stereophonic sound picture.

developed by Alan Blumlein, uses two different polar response patterns. Cardioid, variations of cardioid or omni can be utilised for the centre-facing element of the stereo configuration (Mid or 'sum') and a figure of eight, bidirectional polar response pattern is used for the sides of the image (Side or 'difference'). This technique is in essence encoded stereo as we need to process the information captured via the microphone using a figure of eight pattern to create a separate left and right channel.

MS becomes three-channel stereo, as after decoding you will end up with what amounts to 'LCR', the mid channel being panned to the centre

EQUIVALENCE STEREO (NEAR-COINCIDENT STEREO) OR 'MIXED STEREO'

Many practitioners like using near-coincident techniques because of the SRA they yield. For the most part, techniques such as EBS, ORTF, NOS, DIN and RAI combine level and time differences to create a virtual image over speakers that generally spreads the various sound sources being captured evenly between two speakers. Phantom images are prominent and reproduced sound sources have an element of width while retaining near-accurate localisation.

An experimental recording in which a binaural recording and binaurally encoded recordings captured via a microphone array and soundfield (ambisonics) microphone were compared when capturing movement around a 360-degree soundstage. The microphones used include a binaural dummy head (Neumann KU 100), a Soundfield SPS442B microphone and five DPA 4011 pencil condenser microphones.

The distance between the microphones in these configurations is small enough to consider the level differences as still a measurable and usable way in which to localise a given sound source. In this instance, however, unlike solely coincident configurations, the distance between the microphones offers measurable time of arrival variations at the microphone diaphragms. The level differences are again captured by using microphones with directional polar response patterns and the principle of capturing 'on-' and 'off-axis' variations (level and frequency).

The near-coincident technique arguably provides the best of both worlds (intensity stereophony and time of arrival stereophony). You can attain good localisation of a given sound source or the sources within the soundstage you are recording, while capturing a fairly ambient and expansive sound.

When using any directional microphone as part of a stereo configuration, unfortunately, there is the risk of losing low frequency detail if the arrangement is far away from the source you wish to capture. Omnipolar response patterns used when working with time difference stereo do not suffer in this manner, but localisation accuracy is compromised.

ORTF is a very popular technique as the 17cm spacing between the microphone diaphragms and angle of 110 degrees between the microphones is seen as offering a similar set of time and level difference localisation cues to that of the human ear, albeit without the height or periphonic element of sound. However, how we hear sound and how we measure sound arriving at our ears, for example, localisation purposes is far more complicated. Stereo techniques are used to play back on systems dealing primarily with the horizontal plane.

Baffled stereo can be used to enhance the left and right channel separation and when played back over headphones can work with intensity differences and the nature of waveforms to create a very slight sense of elevation or periphony. As a sound's frequency increases it becomes more directional and can be considered as ray energy, like light, with

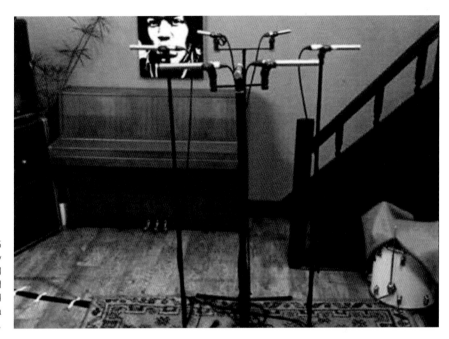

A variation of an INA-5 multi-microphone array using two additional microphones, making a total of seven AKG C451 pencil condensers, for capturing a 360-degree soundstage.

the sound reflecting off surfaces at the specified angle of entry. Low frequency is less directional in nature and is considered as wave energy.

BINAURAL RECORDING

It is worth taking the time to understand the difference between stereophonic and binaural recording. Unlike stereo recording, binaural recording can offer a more immersive listening experience as both lateral and vertical localisation cues are captured and reproduced over headphones. Although there can be some limitations, recordings using this technique may suit very specialist projects and applications.

If you listen back to a binaural recording via speakers the recording retains an element of depth and width but loses the height cues. This is in part because of the increased crosstalk and distance between the speakers, which, unlike headphones, no longer reproduce the same interaural variations at the ear.

Whether a recording is captured using a specialist dummy head with omnidirectional microphones housed in the artificial ears, or by placing microphones in your own ears, such recordings by the very nature of how the microphones are placed will be impacted by the way in which sound, specifically the different frequencies and related wavelengths, resultant waveforms and general propagation of sound, reflects, refracts and diffracts when the acoustic barrier that is the human skull is taken into consideration.

Indeed, alongside interaural time and interaural level differences (ITDs and ILDs) arriving at the microphones housed in the artificial ears, the propagation of sound is varied to say the least. Intensity and spectral differences and the directionality of a given frequency all contribute to how our ears localise a sound source when the human skull acts as an acoustic shadow and barrier between the two ears.

This is a very simplified explanation and there is a vast amount of literature and ongoing research when it comes to sound localisation, related spatial audio considerations, and subsequent applications in the field of recording and reproduction systems. Just looking up head-related transfer

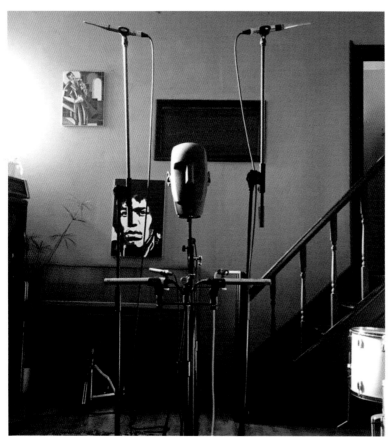

Another experimental recording that again utilises a variation of an INA-5. This has a configuration possibly more resembling a 'Williams Star' alongside an additional pair of microphones to play back through the height layer of a multichannel-based speaker system. Again a binaural dummy head has been used to compare with a binaurally encoded interpretation of what the microphone array had captured.

functions (HRTFs) would be enough to keep you going for the foreseeable future.

Using binaural recording for purposes that are not static, such as a first-person view in a computer game or film, is very effective. Many dummy heads allow for a camera to be attached to the top of the head and when synced with audio such video recordings can make for a very immersive experience. The dummy head and camera, for example, could be wheeled around a live room or stage while a band is performing. For the end user at the reproduction stage, listening back via headphones can be an interesting experience, although no two people hear sound in an identical manner due to variables, some anatomical, such as the shape of the ear.

When using a binaural dummy head you could also move the performers themselves around the head, in essence allowing you to capture a non-static recording of a 360-degree soundstage, although this novel approach would be distracting and without any purpose. VR, AR, gaming and other media arguably benefit from immersive audio. Binaural room scanning also serves a function when, among other uses, it can be utilised to record, measure and, through employing clever algorithms, emulate and map out a virtual listening environment for engineers to use on location.

MULTI-MICROPHONE ARRAYS

This is a hugely specialised field when it comes to recording and the reproduction of sound over multiple speakers, with or without height channels. Again take a look at the work of engineers and practitioners such as Michael Williams, Guillaume Le Dû of Radio France, Günther Theile of the Institut für Rundfunktechnik in Munich and Morten Lindberg of the Norwegian record label 2L. There are many more engineers, authors and researchers who deserve to be mentioned but it was mostly Michael Williams's papers and books that inspired me to experiment with recording using multiple microphones.

In terms of recording there are various arrays for surround and other multichannel-based reproduction systems and configurations such as INA5, Double MS, NHK, PCMA, Polyhymnia Pentagon, Cardioid Trapezoid, Fukada Tree, Decca Cuboid and many others. There are also variations of the 'Wiliams Star' technique and those such as the OCT-3D in which extra layers of microphones are added for reproduction-based systems with height.

In discussing recording for a basic five-channel surround reproduction system via speakers, Michael Williams considers the idea of 'critical linking', by which continuous coverage of a 360-degree soundstage is achieved by the well-considered placement of five microphones. If coverage is broken down into segments, then each segment could be seen as capturing an image of the soundstage based on level and time differences in a similar manner to equivalence stereophony.

The practical difference here is that instead of just having two speakers to contend with in terms of creating a virtual image (stereo recording angle), you are trying to capture five images that can be combined together to provide continuous coverage over a 360-degree soundstage, as opposed to the traditional front-facing soundstage of 180 degrees. This allows for some very creative applications. It is possible, for example, to place all the musicians around an array of this type when recording.

Here room reflections of the various instruments will be captured by all the microphones in the array, which can add a sense of envelopment when listening back over, for example, a five-channel speaker system.

As a starting point try using five condenser microphones with cardioid or hyper-cardioid polar response patterns. Each microphone is then panned to the speaker that represents its relative position within the array: the front left microphone in the array is panned or routed directly to the front left speaker, the microphone at the centre of the array to the centre speaker, and so on. Using microphones with directional patterns in a similar manner to an equivalence stereo technique like DIN, EBS or ORTF allows you to listen and gauge the spread of the sound sources within the captured image over the two speakers in question. You can experiment with using omni- and other polar response patterns.

As this book is only meant to be an introduction to the art of recording, I would recommend undertaking further research if you are interested in the fields of surround and spatial audio.

Some of the most enjoyable recording sessions in which I have been involved have meant experimenting with a variety of arrays in order to capture a 360-degree soundstage. It is just a shame that such recordings are not always accessible, at least in a faithful manner – binaural encoding for playback via headphones has mixed results – as many people do not have access to a well set-up 5.1 system with a controlled listening environment.

When considering recording for specialised media I would recommend looking into the subjects of ambisonics and sphere microphones. Spatial audio has become more of a consideration as delivery systems have become more accessible. Concepts that originate from many years ago are being reimagined and implemented through the application of improved technology and processing, and as a result spatial audio has sometimes become arguably less novel and more of a necessity in terms of facilitating new media in an effective manner.

4

THE BASICS OF RECORDING VOCALS

Capturing a great vocal sound is one of the more difficult challenges for a recording engineer. Depending on the genre and brief, it can be seen as a given that the vocal is going to sit upfront and centre within the listening soundstage and final mix. So sometimes there really is nowhere to hide.

Firstly we need to look at the psychology behind delivering a believable and standout vocal performance.

If a guitarist, drummer or any instrumentalist has a bad day, they can, at least in part, blame the instrument. On many occasions I have heard a guitarist say 'I need new strings' for example, or there is an issue with their pedals or amp. When it comes to a vocalist, however, they have nothing or no one to blame but themselves.

I have had the pleasure of working with some great singers over the years, but if the mood in the studio is not right and the vocalist is not warmed up or not feeling at their best then a tracking session can be an uphill struggle from the outset.

I like to work in an organic and, to me, more fluid manner, alongside a vocalist who is well rehearsed, warmed up and focused enough to get a whole take in one. This is, of course, fanciful on many levels and, in line with modern production tools, has become almost an obsolete concept in some circles.

The idea of dropping in (from a given place within the song) or punching in (a real-time dub), to in effect record a bit at a time and then piece, compile or 'comp' together a master take has become more of the norm for many.

Though this may be the only option, depending on the competency of the performer and the type of project, it can present all sorts of issues in relation to continuity.

Some producers love working on a section, phrase or even one word at a time, as they feel this gives them options or sometimes it can be because they want to focus on a specific word or phrase in terms of telling a story, in which intonation and inflection become a consideration.

There is much to consider when thinking about a vocal part as something close to telling a story. A story that makes the listener aware of deep involvement and feelings, convincingly putting across the passion that the emotional force of many records can inspire. One might expect this of all musicians, but from my experience it can be more difficult when recording and crafting a believable vocal.

In terms of the performance there are many things to take into consideration. The first and possibly most obvious is pitch: is the vocalist in tune? I do not mean to be rude or possibly crass by stating what should be obvious, but like any other instrument you should be aiming to work with competent performers. If I hired a session drummer or saxophonist for a tracking session and they were not well rehearsed or suitable for the style of the project, then from the start I am making life more difficult for myself.

It is not always viable to work with your dream vocalist for many reasons and often you may come across a band whose vocalist is an integral part of the line-up regardless of their ability and singing prowess.

A dynamic microphone, such as the Shure SM7B, can often be ideal for live tracking sessions. Spill is less of a problem than it can be with some of the more sensitive condenser microphones, for example, that are often housed at any given studio, and it sounds great.

Without wanting to cause an argument, I would just recommend being prepared before a recording session. This is why pre-production is so important. If you are not the project manager or the producer, then you should hope that whoever is overseeing that role, which may be the band themselves, is aware that vocals could possibly be the area that needs most work.

It is often about having options and a well thought-out approach concerning how to tackle any issues about pitch before the recording takes place.

Even if you are not the producer or directing the session, a bit of pre-production goes a long way. Does the vocalist always have issues with pitch or is it more noticeable in certain circumstances, such as when on stage? Have they had any training or at least spoken to a vocal coach about warming up exercises?

Singing is in part about projection, which in a very simplified manner pertains to the volume and acoustic resonance of the human voice. It may well be that dynamics and pitch are being impacted because the vocalist is shouting and does not know how to project their voice within the range they are most naturally comfortable. Projection can be improved by looking at posture and breathing, amongst over factors, and therefore

it may be a good idea to politely recommend a vocalist looks into meeting up with a vocal coach before any planned sessions.

This may not be an option, however, and explaining to a vocalist that they do not need to shout to be heard in the studio when using a sensitive microphone can help. They also do not have to compete with lots of background noise, or terrible monitoring. Choosing a suitable pair of headphones and balanced foldback mix for the headphones is imperative when tracking vocals.

A vocalist should not have to overly project their voice and shout if they are not competing with what they are listening to in their cans. You can also suggest that they try wearing only one headphone, so in essence one headphone on and one headphone off. This is not always necessary, though, if you provide a well-balanced foldback mix at appropriate levels so that the vocalist can hear their voice in context and not at such high sound pressure levels that they push themselves out of their range.

You should also try to provide the recording artist with the most direct path in terms of monitoring. In many studios this is facilitated by using the aux buses as 'cue' sends before the converters. If you have to send the vocals being tracked into the artist's headphones post converters and are having issues with latency, with the vocalist hearing a lag or delay in their headphones, then you can either try reducing the buffer size in your DAW or bounce out the backing track (balanced to the artist's preference). You can then start a new session, just using the bounced stereo backing track as a reference for monitoring and tracking. This can be helpful if you are working in the box and have a large session that you have already started, editing, mixing and processing the audio that constitutes what we have been referring to as the 'backing track'.

Many modern audio interfaces give an option of direct monitoring. Making sure there is no problematic audible delay or lag in the performer's headphones is vital, not least because it can be very distracting for them.

A big part of vocal tracking is the timing and phrasing. When working on recording one section at a time, this can be very difficult to edit together during post-production or on the 'fly'.

In this context one consideration concerning phrasing directly relates to how the vocals are delivered and land in relation to the rest of the music: does it flow and sound effortless or is it rigid, out of time, characterless and anything but fluid? Articulation and dynamics need to be considered, as well as onsets (how breath and the vocal cords work together at the attack, the start of the note) and offsets (how a note finishes).

There is much more to this and as always I would advise undertaking further research, but from a recording engineer's point of view, as you can imagine, the unrehearsed, unprepared stop-start approach to a vocal tracking session can be problematic for many reasons, even with a well-trained vocalist and a great set-up at your disposal.

As usual there are different ways in which to approach and facilitate recording. What does not work for one artist and style of vocal may well work for another. Tracking rhythmical rhyme and rapping has a different flow to that of an opera singer. Projection, dynamics, articulation and modulation should all likely be considered in a completely different manner as well.

Many engineers recommend sending a little bit of reverb to an artist's headphones to help them relax, and to help with pitching (though there are many differing opinions here), but this really depends again on what and who you are tracking, because for an artist who is not considering pitch as their main focus and wants to concentrate instead on the mood, rhythm and timing, reverb can be off-putting when focusing on the attack and how they land on a given beat.

You may also find that when you choose a condenser or a particularly sensitive ribbon microphone an inexperienced vocalist can be put off and surprised by the detail they hear in their headphones. On this occasion a little bit of subtle reverb to soften the sound can be very useful.

However, it is worth mentioning here that it is worth using a bus to send to your reverb. If you are going to record this reverb, do so on a separate channel so you always have the clean and dry vocal to work with at a later date.

On that note I always get asked about the amount of vocal processing I use at the recording stage. This depends on many factors, such as the type of vocal being recorded, the quality of the vocalist and the control they have in terms of dynamics. The room acoustics and quality of the equipment I am working with and how many channels I have to play with are all considerations.

If you are in a studio with a treated live room and a balanced reverberation characteristic, then you can work with acoustic energy and move a vocalist further away from a microphone to attain a more balanced and natural tone without worrying about the room colouring the sound in an unfavourable manner, or any loss of intelligibility when you pass the point of critical distance, which may be a problem in a larger untreated space such as a church or concert hall.

Working with such a reverberated sound may be good for a concert, with a microphone mainly being used for sound reinforcement and the room's acoustics doing a lot of the work in terms of assisting with vocal projection, while adding ambience and character to a performance by a choir or opera singer, for example. It can also be useful, however, to work in a more controlled environment such as a large treated live room in order to really take control and shape a vocal performance during post-production.

On such occasions as when I am recording a very dynamic performance, the sort an opera singer might deliver for example, then I am not looking at restricting the performance in terms of dynamics. I do not always use compression, at least not for any major dynamic processing, and am more focused on the size and sound of the room. I definitely would not consider placing the microphone close to the artist either, as this can impact the tone and distort the sound.

Subtle spatial and dynamic processing may be applied during post, but the latter is often mainly to bring out some of the less discernible and quieter parts of the performance. Even then, however, this approach is not necessary if you get the performance and recording you desire at the source.

Live guide vocal recording. A live guide is when the vocalist sings along in real time, often to help the musicians tracking gauge dynamics and, for example, give a sense of where they are in the arrangement. Here a Shure SM7B dynamic microphone is being used.

By contrast, if you record in a smaller room with too much treatment, specifically foam, as that seems to be fashionable, and the absorption rate increases to the point that the room sounds anechoic (not as bad as an anechoic chamber, just without discernible reflections or acoustic energy), then you will lose a lot of the high-end frequencies in your recordings and they will lack tonal balance with the low-mids normally being prominent in the sound. I would go further here and suggest that close microphone technique in general, when applied in a room treated to such a degree that one would describe it as sounding 'dead' (lacking reflections and the build-up of reverberant sound) is far from ideal for any acoustic instrument or the voice, as it will impact the initial build-up of sound energy. This is not something you can add later, specifically in terms of natural acoustic energy.

Choosing the space to record in is really important. From a budget perspective, as long as room reflections are controlled to a certain extent in the vicinity of the microphone you are using, then some good results can be achieved. Many companies have designed various affordable enclosures for exactly this purpose, such as the Reflexion Filter range by sE Electronics.

Even if you have a great sounding room to work with, it is often desirable to get a close and intimate sound by moving the vocalist closer to the microphone. Sometimes engineers position acoustic baffle boards around the vocalist to alter the sound or place the artist in a purpose-built vocal booth. Acoustic diffusors on castors can also be moved to create an enclosure around the chosen microphone(s) to manipulate reflections and specific frequencies in order to colour and enhance the sound being recorded at source.

I find that processing at the recording stage is normally more of a creative consideration than corrective. Granted applying a subtle amount of downward compression to tame the odd peak is corrective, but I often use various compressors for additional tone shaping in conjunction with the preamps and EQ, if applied. Depending on how the compressor grabs the audio, the processing of transients can really help shape a sound and give the impression that a vocal is larger than life and upfront, and when needed is able to cut and punch through a mix in a rhythmical manner. I should warn you, however, that dynamic processing in any shape or form can really spoil a recording.

Often when starting out it is best to work with a vocalist and get them to learn some microphone technique, such as where to place their mouth to get the most appropriate tone and when to move away from the microphone, although in some circumstances the latter can cause issues with continuity. You can also find a middle point where the microphone will not be overloaded in loud passes or sound too distant in quieter passages, or ride a fader to alter the recording level instead of using inappropriate compression and run the risk of being stuck with a squashed, misshaped sound or pumping effect.

Though continuity is again a potential issue when editing different takes together, one of the benefits of recording section by section is that you can adjust the positioning of the vocalist in relation to the microphone.

If you are going to use compression, edge on the side of caution and look at perhaps no more than a couple of decibels in gain reduction and listen to how it sounds and reacts to the performance. The main thing is to adjust how fast the compressor reacts and realigns to any incoming transient. Compression can be applied in a manner that complements the performance articulation. It can be musical and complement the shape and delivery of what is being recorded, whether that involves fast transients or slow and sustained notes, for example.

Often in studios you will have access to multiple channels and therefore you can get the best of both worlds. For instance, I may record the vocal with a microphone that suits the vocalist after performing a 'shootout' to decide which one compliments their voice. Then, room acoustics permitting, I may move the singer to various distances from the microphone and listen to find a sweet spot.

I will parallel the vocal channel either via a designated 'parallel' point on the patchbay or an insert send on the channel, and then return the duplicate signal to a separate channel. This channel can then be processed and recorded separately. As touched upon earlier, you may wish to bus some reverb to the artist's headphones. The reverb, or more specifically the channel the wet sound is returning on, whether via hardware or otherwise, should ideally be routed to record on a separate channel.

Not only does this give you options, but by sending a hyped sound after processing to the artist's foldback you can often influence their performance. After all, if they sound like a superhero in their cans, they may well perform like one.

Tips for vocalists starting out

When a vocalist is new to studio recording, potentially inexperienced and nervous, don't shove a really sensitive microphone in front of them, send the foldback mix to their headphones and expect them to perform in a manner that is natural to their performance ability. It can often be good to use a cheaper dynamic alongside (placed coincident) a more sensitive ribbon or condenser microphone. Send the signal from the dynamic to their headphones as this can be less off-putting. You can record with the ribbon or condenser at the same time and choose to process the signal at the source, it's up to you, but ideally the vocalist should not back off as much after hearing things they are not used to in their cans.

Do not use a pop shield simply to minimise plosives, but use it to set a distance at which you want the vocalist to stand away from the microphone. Inexperienced vocalists tend to move around and on occasion can get too close when using very sensitive microphones. Microphone technique, in terms of how a vocalist works with the microphone to articulate themselves and create certain nuances, is an art in itself.

Like many engineers I find it best to record vocals, job permitting, when I can send an edited or, if I am both producing and mixing, a near-mixed version of the project into the artist's headphones.

If you are recording a live performance with little time to prepare and cannot mix the sounds in any meaningful and practical way at the recording stage using a console and outboard, for example, then providing a mix akin to what some call 'ear candy' (a pleasing mix) can be a challenge. If you are tracking the vocals at a later stage in the production process, however, and have the option it makes sense. Think about it – how can you ask a vocalist to focus on timing, phrasing, tuning and everything else if the backing track is unbalanced and just messy in so many ways.

What you send to a performer's headphones and the overall foldback balance and mix is important.

PLOSIVES AND FRICATIVES

SIBILANTS

Sibilant sounds occur roughly within the 4–10KHz frequency range (give or take). The common phonetic or pronunciation of sound associated with sibilance is a hissing sound heard principally with the letters 's' and 'z'. The unwanted 'shh' and 'ess' sounds can be problematic on many levels. In the first instance I would recommend undertaking a microphone shootout, if possible, as some microphones will reduce such issues at the source depending on the unique character of the vocalist in question in relation to the frequency and transient response of the microphone. Altering the polar response pattern and moving a directional microphone can have an impact on tonal quality, but often it requires a totally different microphone to hear a noticeable difference when it comes to reducing sibilance.

You can try moving the artist away from the microphone, but again this is not always a solution in its own right and you may find yourself reaching

for a 'de-esser' tool, which is effectively a dynamic EQ that attenuates a targeted and problematic set of frequencies.

PLOSIVES (OCCLUSIVE)

I always ask my students to put a hand in front of their mouth and alternate saying words beginning with the letter 'P' and those with other letters. You can also work your way through the alphabet and notice fluctuations in air pressure, albeit to a lesser extent depending on the person, with letters such as 'b', 'd', 'k' and 't'. In practical terms consonants with 'pa', 'ba' and 'fa' sounds can be the most problematic.

In the simplest of explanations, in audio recording plosives are an issue when distortion is audible in the form of sudden 'pops'. These occur when a sudden burst of air, due to the airflow being blocked, hits the often sensitive diaphragm of a microphone when recording vocals.

Using a pop shield placed in front of the microphone can help to reduce such distortions. They can also help you provide a good working distance between the microphone and artist if you are happy with a given sound and do not wish the vocalist to get any closer to the microphone.

Moving an artist further away from a very sensitive microphone can help with reducing plosives if you have decent acoustics to work with. Otherwise you can use a high pass filter (HPF), dynamic EQ or, in some circumstances, use your chosen DAW to zoom in and process/render out the offending frequencies just on the offending onset of a given word.

MONITORING

It is very important to spend some serious time considering the headphone (foldback) mix. Latency, or the delay that can audibly manifest when using a digital signal chain/flow, if it's your only choice, can have a negative impact on the performance, not least issues with timing and phrasing. If you do not have a set-up where you can send the signal back to the artist's headphone pre-converters, then try reducing the buffer size in your DAW.

If this is a problem, bounce out what you have been working on and start a new session, using just a well-balanced stereo (or mono) file to work with solely for tracking. Ideally I like to give my vocalists a near-finished mix or at least something like ear candy to work with. Vocalists should not have to compete with issues of timing and tuning in regards to the instruments and music already recorded unless it is a live performance, in which case, as with all instruments, it is about getting a great sound at source with plenty of headroom.

You should also start with very low levels in the cans and try to work with the artist to find a happy balance. A telltale sign of a foldback mix being unbalanced and too loud is when vocalists drift out of tune because they are competing with the level of the headphone mix in order to hear themselves, and subsequently by pushing themselves in an uncontrolled manner they can end up singing out of their range.

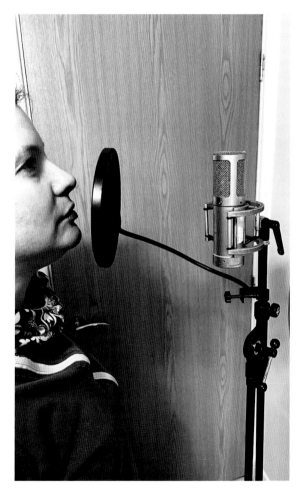

Though these pictures are not highlighting any particular placement or what might be considered as 'best practice', it can be a good starting point to have the artist's mouth level with the microphone diaphragm and 'on axis' if using a directional polar pattern. Omnipolar patterns and a little distance between the artist and microphone can help gauge the vocalist's microphone technique and the suitability of a given microphone. If you are going to use a directional polar response pattern, experiment with on- and off-axis positioning to alter the tone. You can also get close to a microphone with a directional polar response pattern to experiment with the proximity effect, something that can be useful with beat boxing. In this photo a Brauner Phantom V large diaphragm condenser microphone is being used alongside a pop shield.

It can often be a case of using EQ to rebalance the spectral aspect of the foldback mix as certain frequencies can be very fatiguing and restricting when a vocalist is placed in an enclosed listening environment, such as when using closed-back and noise-isolating headphones.

As always when it comes to the equipment used for monitoring, there is no 'one size fits all' scenario and you have to experiment. Some vocalists enjoy the openness of open-back headphones, but these can cause issues with bleed, some like to use the 'one ear on, one ear off' technique, and some artists like to work with speakers rather than any headphones in

Microphone shoot-out. It can be useful to compare different microphones when working with a vocalist you have not worked with before. Trying to get a great sound at source is key, so that the engineer and/or producer can then focus on the performance.

Recording vocals in stereo using the Blumlein, MS or XY techniques can be very effective, especially if the artist has a habit of moving around. It is best to use intensity/level difference stereo techniques whereby the microphones are placed coincident to one another to minimise issues pertaining to destructive interference when down-mixed to mono. Here an AEA R88 stereo ribbon microphone is being used alongside a pop shield.

the first instance. Often overseeing a headphone shootout can be useful if you know you will be potentially working for long hours, especially when another aspect to consider involves keeping a session flowing once a vocalist has warmed up their voice.

It is also worth considering what actually needs to be in the mix, depending on what type of vocals are being recorded. If, for example, it's a case of laying down rhythmical rhyme and rapping on a track, then the artist may want more of the drums and rhythm section in their cans. If it is a very sustained melodic performance, then the artist may wish to have more of the melodic aspects of the arrangement sounding in the foldback mix.

When working in unison to thicken up and layer sounds in different octaves or laying down harmonies, you may also need to alter what the artist needs to hear in order to help them with pitch when focusing on a given part.

I have known producers use audio cues in a similar manner to when ADR is overseen during post-production for film. If a vocalist is struggling with coming in at the correct place, additional audio cues, such as a click or the sound of a cowbell, are placed on the time line and make an appropriate sound to tell the artist when to come in. In a well-prepared session such cues can be mapped into the project before the session begins.

Tips from a vocologist

Kaya Herstad Carney, who combines the roles of a vocal health habilitation professional, vocologist, vocal arranger/producer, musical director, singer/songwriter and vocal coach, has a number of suggestions:

My main priorities when getting ready for a studio session as a vocalist or singer/songwriter is to ensure we are all on the same page. Reference tracks can be key to this, but also communicating clearly what you are going for. The process is, of course, different as a session singer than as a feature artist, but I always try to follow these guidelines in preparation and during studio sessions:

Pre-session
- Make sure everything is well rehearsed and that you already know the emotional journey of the song;
- Agree on reference tracks with the producer/band/team;
- Get a good night's sleep;
- Avoid spicy food, alcohol and dairy products;
- Don't exhaust your voice in the days leading up to the session;
- Try not to schedule more than 4–5 hours, especially for lead vocals.

Day of session
- Drink sufficient water;
- Warm up with SOVT (semi-occluded vocal tract) exercises, which are resistance exercises that help balance the airflow with the vocal folds and promote efficient and agile vocals;
- Sing the song through a couple of times to test the dynamic performance, making sure that the overall journey of the vocal throughout the whole performance works with the headroom of the mic;
- Get the right microphone for the sound you're going for and the correct placement (for example, do you want one with bass tip up, or a 'proximity effect' via a close mic, or to obtain more of a room sound);
- Get the mood right for the song, perhaps by turning down the lighting, closing your eyes or even the complete opposite, making sure there are people in the studio to perform to;
- Get the monitor (foldback) mix right. Reverb can help with the feel, but can also have a negative effect on the tuning. Intonation is also more difficult if bass frequencies are dominating what the singer can hear;
- Take regular breaks;
- Check in with the team to hear their notes, but ensure all notes given are positive and actionable, rather than personal and descriptive;
- Get all the integral/main parts down before moving on to background vocals, ad libs and other potential ideas.

5
RECORDING DRUMS

In this chapter we will discuss different techniques and thought processes concerning how you can record a drum kit. The key thing to remember from the outset, however, is that

Cole 4038 classic ribbon microphone being used as a room microphone placed at the side of the kit.

once again there really is no single solution that suits all production styles or a given brief. Some of the greatest players have amazing dynamics and can balance their own performances with or without decent monitoring, such as foldback. In that case, if you have a well-tuned drum kit and a great-sounding room in which a specific part of the kit doesn't need to be enhanced or manipulated during post production, it can be argued that using fewer microphones with some strategic placement will capture a great sound.

On the other hand, less experienced players may need the assistance of the engineer in balancing their performance within a mix, and it may be better to use more microphones to capture each part of the drum kit in order to increase the options available if it is necessary to alter a recording. The engineer, for example, may prefer or need to apply corrective or creative editing techniques. This can be problematic when a drum kit is recorded more as a whole instrument to create an overall sound, using fewer microphones positioned at a distance.

ANATOMY OF A BASIC 5-PIECE DRUM KIT

Drums come in many different shapes and sizes. There are also many different types of cymbals and a host of accessories that can help a drummer craft a specific sound.

Drums on a modern kit generally have two heads (sometimes referred to as drum skins): the 'batter head' (top) and the 'resonant head' (bottom).

Drum shells (basic)
Bass drum
Snare drum
Rack tom
Second rack tom
Floor tom

Cymbals (basic)
Hi-hat
Crash
Ride

I have always loved recording drums, in part because I am a drummer myself, but also because it is one of those many opportunities in recording where multiple approaches and hybrid techniques can yield a variety of results. In a nutshell, you can get creative and it is no longer just about capturing a performance.

Many people will place microphones around a drum kit or record various percussion instruments in order to capture samples. Whether it is single hits, loops or some other sound generated within a given space, these sounds can be loaded into a sampler and utilised in many ways as part of both corrective and creative practice.

You can also alter the tone and resonance of drums in many ways, as with any other acoustic instrument. You could, for example, place tea towels on the drum skins or apply various gels (toilet roll, tape and so on) to dampen a given drum. Or you can add resonance and tone by adding another kick drum in front of the existing kick drum. Some drummers and percussionists attach chains or apply other treatments to create rattles and various sound effects. You can tape bits of thin plastic to a bass (kick) drum skin near where the beater hits to add extra 'slap' to the sound. As we will find in Chapter 7, there are many ways to create acoustic excitation through the process of re-amping and placing speakers near to drums (or any other hollow and resonant chamber or instrument).

Experiment, experiment, listen back and then experiment some more.

When it comes to recording drums, microphone choice, technique and placement is all about one word, and is related to one concern for many practitioners. This word is 'options'. For producers, mix engineers and those involved at the post-production stage, choice is very important.

One microphone can capture a good overall sound, but such a recording can lack any real detail and in practice it narrows our options regarding what can be done with such a recording. This detail can be down to many factors, such as the localisation of a sound and how big that recorded sound is within the listening soundstage.

How would the listener discern where any given drum is positioned if only one microphone was used? Placing one microphone closer to a particular drum or cymbal gives the sense that the drum or cymbal is close to the listener and louder. You could also attain a sense of depth, or more accurately distance, if the same microphone is positioned further away. If the microphone is close to the drum kit or percussion instrument then in theory it sounds less roomy. However, if the microphone is placed at a distance, one would expect the recording to sound more like the room the kit is being recorded in.

Depending on the size of the room and its reverberation characteristic, the ratio between the close and upfront, direct sound of the instrument would eventually be overtaken by the sound and ambience of the room. (*See* 'critical distance' in the Glossary, although such a concept is easier to associate and picture with fairly large and reverberant spaces.)

How noticeable the reverberation is, both in terms of the time it takes to decay away (RT60) and at what frequencies the reverberation is most noticeable, depends on the size and materials of the room chosen for the recording. Practitioners often choose to use close microphone techniques to minimise spill for control purposes in post-production, and because they do not like the sound of the room and how it colours the overall recorded sound unfavourably.

In order to localise where a sound source is within a particular space, you should use multiple microphones in a specific array, at the very least a stereo microphone technique that captures time and intensity differences, which on playback provide the listener with varying interaural time and level differences. However, if you are not 100 per cent concerned with stereophonic (stereographic) information and the localisation of a given sound source within the listening soundstage, you can use a mixture of close and ambient microphones. Where you place the musicians within a live room or particular space to record can be a good way to open up the listening soundstage and arguably make a recorded sound or performance appear bigger, or possibly more specifically wider.

Working with spill, in which the sound of one instrument is captured by a microphone positioned to capture another instrument performing in the same room, can be an effective way to open up the sound of a recording.

It is worth listening to many early recordings, especially when it comes to jazz. It is often about the drummer being dynamic in their performance and able to balance the sound of the drum kit themselves when they are playing. In such recordings fewer microphones are generally used and strategically placed in a good-sounding room with acoustic energy, but controlled to attain a fairly flat reverberation characteristic.

Such minimal, but well-placed, microphones can with some practice capture a good overall sound, tone and, more specifically perhaps, spectral balance of the drums. In such an approach the drum kit is seen and captured in a similar manner to many other acoustic instruments in that it is recorded as one whole instrument, as opposed to being seen as many separate parts.

Many practitioners use multiple microphones for this very reason. The drum kit – a fairly new instrument in terms of the history of percussion instruments – can be viewed as comprising many individual parts and percussion instruments in their own right, which are combined to create the overall sound and desired pattern.

I often find that many students who have worked solely with MIDI and samples to program and edit drum parts have concerns when it comes to issues such as spill and feel that separation of sound is key to crafting a given production. For this multiple microphones positioned close to each component of a drum kit would be vital. In my view that is not so, but as always it is a choice and for many engineers it is all about functionality and options. As always, it really depends on the brief, but overall I have come to believe that less really can be more when it comes to using microphones and crafting the particular production aesthetic I have in mind.

Arguably such minimal approaches are just not suitable in some instances. In specialist recordings for surround sound and channel-based systems, for example, where periphony or sound with height is taken into considerations, large numbers of microphones can be employed in various array configurations.

A practitioner may also need to capture a specific element of a kit for further creative processing during the mix stage. When an engineer wants to manipulate sound after a recording, aiming for less spill and trying to isolate various transients of a wanted sound becomes more of a technical focus than a musical one, at least at the recording stage.

But let us get back to the basics. I recommend trying to find a decently sized space, such as an old church or school hall, to record in and experiment recording a few musicians playing only acoustic instruments. It works well if the instruments are varied not only in timbre and sound, but in the level of SPLs they create. Drums, for example, will naturally be louder when hit with sticks then an acoustic guitar.

Stick to using no more than one microphone per instrument and, if the room has a noticeable amount of reverb, ideally try spacing the musicians out.

Although I recommend mixing with speakers for many reasons, using headphones in such a recording session is fine, and in this instance we are listening for a different type of balance too when mixing or capturing a specific type of recorded performance. It is about listening to the room and the character of the sounds of each instrument within that room. Ultimately it is about what balance, if any, you can produce by placing just a few microphones, and how the performance dynamics of the musicians will impact the balance of the room's sound.

In this example the microphone closer to the drum kit may well capture an element of detail with some subtle colouring, courtesy of the reverberation characteristic, and the other microphone placed further away in the room to capture the other instruments adds a noticeable acoustic energy and character, a reverberation characteristic that reacts to the dynamics of the performance. The short delay introduced from microphones placed elsewhere in the room also adds a sense of depth and of subtle width (if panned). The louder the drummer plays and the more the room acoustics are altered by these changes in SPLs, the more the microphones at the other side of the room alter in terms of the ratio of spill and the sounds they have been set up to capture.

This approach really helped me attain a better sense of where to place microphones when it came to recording live performances, but it also helped me become more creative in my approach to recording drums. I often found that when recording a trio of drums, bass and piano, the record became less static and more interesting when I incorporated spill in a creative manner and tried not to fight against it. Though I am not suggesting that I have any full understanding of how 'Take Five' (Columbia Records, 1959), performed by the Dave Brubeck Quartet and written by its saxophonist Paul Desmond, was recorded, it is well worth a listen to hear what can be achieved with minimal microphones, excellent musicians and a great sounding space. I would also humbly suggest that I have often been very pleased with spill that has been used for effect after having been captured by one or more microphones set up to record other instruments elsewhere in a large live room, an effect akin to that heard during the drum solo in 'Take Five'.

No doubt Teo Macero, the producer, would have focused on the performance first and foremost, but when it comes to a recording of this nature it is not often about lots of microphones. Instead, it is about placement, listening and balancing the sound being captured, and again spill can be very useful. I cite this track purely because when recording trios I have often attained really interesting sounds from drums reflecting off a piano lid and into a nearby microphone, for example. Such creative occurrences tend to come to fruition when a performer is playing a solo and riding into such spill can really open up the listening soundstage.

When we discuss balance as a recording engineer, it can also refer to the spectral balance of the combined picture of sound we are creating and how this is spread over the listening soundstage. In the case of a jazz trio of upright bass, piano and drums, it may be that the more sustained and resonant bass notes are sent to both speakers, whereas the drums are panned mainly into one speaker, with some very low sub frequencies filtered out, and the piano is then panned into the other speaker. This can emphasise separation, but overall a nice balance is created in terms of the overall picture of sound being presented via the speakers. Some of this panning and placement came about from the practicalities of routing signals to early tape machines and the limitations of working in mono, but to this day considered panning, based on listening to the frequency range of a set of instruments in order to create that balanced reproduced picture of sound, is an art.

I recall a mastering engineer asking me on one occasion whether I had intended to position my drums (the kit as one whole instrument as opposed to many separate parts) over to the left-hand side of the stereo mix. My answer was simply, yes. No mistake had been made, to me it was just what sounded best at the time of recording.

Microphone spill and drum placement

I have often found that rather than trying to control or minimise spill in the recording situations where you do not have a choice, for example when recording in a large space without acoustic partitions (baffle boards), it is better to ride into the spill and embrace it. Either place the musicians in different spaces to attain a different overall balance of the sounds being recorded in relation to the spill or set up more microphones to capture more of the sounds blending as a whole within the room. The latter with some practice can be used as a sort of crossover.

MICROPHONE TECHNIQUE

Capturing a moment in time and how you choose to record are two very different concepts. This difference is relevant to everything we have discussed so far, so perhaps we should ask ourselves two questions at the start of any recording session: 'what are we trying to capture?' followed closely by 'how are we going to best capture it?' This could be a performance captured, warts and all, with all its glorious imperfections.

Alternatively it could be the quest for perfection, whatever that may be. So how do we set about the recording, or rather what is the recording process best suited to the brief at hand?

Do you want to capture a performance all in one take or something that is recorded in sections over multiple takes, in which case they can be edited together at the post-production stage.

You could, of course, record multiple takes of a full performance and still compile a master take from such performances at a later stage of the record production process.

Then there are other questions to ask, especially when recording an instrument like an acoustic drum kit. For instance, what sort of control do you want over the drum kit in terms of how you wish

to manipulate, enhance, balance and place the various elements that make up a drum kit within the listening soundstage at the time of capturing the sound sources or during post? There are many questions you can ask, but ultimately it all boils down to what sort of production you or the producer/project manager has in mind.

This may sound like common sense, but many people do not approach recording a drum kit seeing it as one whole instrument. A great many of my students have come from a background of working 'in the box', so to speak, with samples and software instruments, and often think of a kick drum, snare drum and hi-hat as being totally separated. As a result, when you discuss the idea of spill and additional resonance, the latter being in part related to the acoustic excitation and in turn the resonance of a rack tom, for example, via the kick or snare when it is not being played, the concept can be quite unfamiliar.

Just because the toms are not being played does not mean they do not have an impact on the overall sound of the drums being played. From this approach the kit is in essence a whole instrument. You can, of course, take away various parts of the kit if they are not being played to see how this impacts the overall sound.

Some producers and engineers ask drummers to alternate how they play in order to attain more separation. This may be simply to ask the player to leave out the cymbals and put down the main back beat of kick and snare with the occasional tom fill. Then the hats and cymbals are overdubbed. This is not a practical way to work in many circumstances, however, not least when a drummer may be playing very intricate parts with lots of ghost notes. Asking them to break up how they play is possibly akin to tying one arm behind their back.

One of the biggest factors is choosing the right tools for the job and making sure that they are in good working order. Are the dimensions of the drums producing the spectral balance, tone and resonance you desire? A tiny kids' toy kit may not be exactly what you are looking for if you want a deep, full-bodied low end resonance to your kick drum sound (though it may sound great in other parts of a production).

Do you want the drums to be resonant and ring out or do you need to dampen them? Is the kick pedal using a soft beater when you really want more of a present attack and click?

As mentioned above, you can dampen the snare drum or toms with something as simple as a tea towel or put a heavy coat on the bass drum.

You can use tape to stick a bit of plastic, such as a credit card, to the part of the skin where the beater hits the drum. Experiment!

The most problematic issues are normally related to tuning and the room acoustics, namely the RT60 time and actual reverberation characteristic, especially if you are only using one microphone or any number of stereo techniques at some distance from the kit. Using fewer microphones

Placement with one microphone

If you only have one microphone to play with, try positioning the microphone about a foot above the right-hand shoulder of the drummer pointing towards the centre of the snare drum (if the drummer uses a right-handed drum set-up). This places it just off to the left of the floor tom, raised up from the floor to be just above or around the head height of the drummer and facing towards the centre of the snare (or kick). It does not need to be exact, as you can always play around with it.

I recommend using either a ribbon or a condenser microphone. If you have access to a condenser microphone with variable polar response patterns, try an omnidirectional polar pattern. This is a good starting point as the frequency response is flatter than a directional polar pattern with off-axis variations, but you could always experiment with a cardioid or figure of eight polar response pattern.

Ideally the microphone should have a good signal to noise ratio (here as it applies to the design build of the microphone), as all electrons flowing as a current can be potentially noisy. Though the ratio of the wanted drum sounds would be far louder than the 'self-noise' of the microphone in most cases, the problem occurs at a later stage when a practitioner may want to use upward compression as an effect or to create some dynamic cohesion between the different drums being played as part of the performance.

The case may be that extreme processing raises the noise floor to a point where it no longer sounds interesting in a 'lo-fidelity' sort of way and just becomes unusable.

You can experiment by sticking the single microphone anywhere you fancy: some engineers place a microphone near to the skin where the beater hits the bass drum or even near the drummers's crotch. It all depends on whatever you think sounds good.

An AKG C414 microphone set to an omnidirectional polar response pattern and placed between the floor tom and snare, near to the bass drum batter head.

provides fewer options in terms of how the engineer can control and manipulate the sound.

However, if you put the time in to tune the kit before the recording and choose a room that complements the performance sound in relation to the production aesthetic you are trying to capture and achieve, less really can be more.

A popular and effective technique, arguably one that should be considered as a basic, is the Glyn Johns Technique, named after the engineer who was credited with developing the method to record drums for many different bands, including the Beatles. If you have not already done so, I recommend watching Peter Jackson's documentary series *The Beatles: Get Back* (2021), in which Glyn Johns makes an appearance.

There are variations of the technique in terms of placement and the occasional addition of extra microphones, for example one on the snare, but one microphone is usually placed in front of the bass drum, one about 1.2m above the centre of the kit, usually the snare, with a third placed to the side of the floor tom at an equal distance from the centre point, the snare. More specifically, ensure the microphone off to the side is a suitable distance from the floor tom's rim facing the centre of the snare drum. I use the word 'suitable' because there are no specific measurements. It's all about the sound of the room, choice of microphones, gain staging, signal processing and, perhaps most pertinently, the quality of the drummer balancing their own performance in terms of dynamics. Once again it is about using your ears and referencing other recordings. Do you like what you are hearing and does it fit the production brief?

The idea of positioning the microphones at an equal difference from the centre of the kit is to help minimise issues that to an extent are related to destructive interference when the signals are summed together. This destructive interference pertains to the phase cycles or, more specifically, the phase coherence when multiple signals are added together. Panning is also taken into consideration. If you choose a centre point to measure from, then applying partial panning to one channel alongside another channel with varied amounts of panning to taste can help with the overall picture and image cohesion of the sound.

Although 100 per cent phase coherence is impossible when recording a source with multiple microphones, and arguably always is without

The Glyn Johns technique. An additional microphone can be added and placed close to the snare drum. Engineers can then keep the snare and kick panned to the centre and slightly pan the microphone placed above the kit, while panning the microphone placed facing the snare from the side of the floor tom slightly more to the left or right. Depending on perspective, this can open up the overall image of the kit.

Two Shure SM57 dynamic microphones positioned top and bottom of the snare drum. Remember to flip/invert the polarity on the channel into which the microphone underneath the snare is plugged.

doctoring the waveforms (*see* Chapter 8), one thing to consider with the microphones used in many techniques is to try to ensure the various signals arrive at the microphone diaphragms with similar phase angles, or more specifically at similar points of a given phase shift. Similar polarities ultimately complement one another and the overall sound when summed together.

This allows for a fuller sound (less frequency cancellation) and can reduce issues with the image being distorted in more complex techniques that use a combination of specific stereo and mono techniques, although this is in part related to time of arrival differences.

Phase coherence becomes far more of an issue as the number of microphones used on a given sound source increases. You are in effect using multiple microphones to capture multiple changes in air pressure emanating directly from a given drum or cymbal at any one time. Each

microphone will capture not only the sound of that drum, regardless of its relative positioning, but also room reflections and other facets.

Every microphone has a different frequency response and transient response. The time of arrival at each microphone is also different. This means that the chances of phase cycles being in relative harmony or sync in terms of phase angles and polarity is slim, not least because it is theoretically impossible to get phase coherence correct when recording in the acoustic domain. Good luck trying to take diffuse, uncorrelated sound propagation into consideration within a room.

It is about minimising audible artefacts, such as a noticeable loss of low end frequency. Is something sounding 'thinner', for want of a better word? Does it lack low end body, bass and resonance?

While learning about microphone placement and experimenting with how to capture the sound of a drum performance, play with the polarity switch

A variation of an AB spaced pair, time of arrival stereo configuration using two Coles 4038 ribbon microphones with bidirectional figure of eight polar response patterns. The snare is used as the centre point to measure from, with the two microphones at an equal distance from it. In this instance the microphones are ever so slightly off axis in terms of facing the centre of the snare.

on the mixing console or stand-alone microphone preamplifier, or via a plugin at the post-production stage (this will be considered in more detail in Chapter 8, alongside image distortion). If you do not have access to a switch to invert polarity, then rewiring the pins in an XLR cable is an option.

Flipping the polarity is a quick and easy way to check whether two or more signals captured via your microphones are complementing one another in terms of the overall phase relationship. By flipping such a switch, you will clearly hear when there is an issue.

A good starting point would be when two microphones are facing one another, something that

An AEA R88 stereo ribbon microphone used as an overhead microphone. Here the engineer can easily switch between using MS and Blumlein intensity stereo or 'level difference' stereo. The microphone acts as a pressure gradient transducer and houses two aluminium ribbon diaphragms mounted at an angle of 90 degrees to one another.

Two AKG C451 B pencil condensers with cardioid polar response patterns placed in a coincident manner to create an XY90 intensity stereo technique. The configuration can be positioned so that the centre of the virtual image created over speakers or SRA is focused on the snare or, as in this example, the centre of the kick drum.

occurs when recording engineers decide to place a microphone facing the top drum skin of a snare, while simultaneously placing one directly below the snare, aiming upwards towards the bottom drum skin to capture the sound of the snare. Some practitioners place microphones above and below toms or use a microphone underneath a hi-hat. The latter can yield interesting results if you are

A DIN equivalence (near coincident) mixed stereo configuration. Again the centre point in-between the configuration is facing towards the centre of the kick drum and could be easily moved to face the centre of the snare. This configuration can provide a less centred image in terms of spreading the overall sound of the drums in-between or at the sides, bunching towards the left and right speakers. Instead the SRA can yield an evenly spread sound of the cymbals and various elements of the drums as a whole over the stereo image.

Multiple techniques can be used to capture the sound of the drum kit. Equivalence stereo, in this case a DIN configuration, is being utilised to capture a stereo image of the overall kit within the room, alongside various microphones placed close to the individual drums to reinforce various elements of the kit, attempt to reduce spill between the various drums and capture less of the room sound.

Both the rack tom and floor tom are being captured via Sennheiser MD 421 dynamic microphones. The microphones are placed away from the drum so as not to impede the player. Together with switching in a low frequency roll-off on the microphone itself, the close positioning in terms of the angle in relation to the axis point and a distance of around 7cm can be a good starting point before looking at any corrective or creative spectral and/or dynamic processing. As always it is paramount that tuning and dampening is considered first.

not having much luck with the more traditional on- or off-axis positioning of a condenser or ribbon microphone placed above the hi-hats.

If the microphones are facing in opposite directions there is a strong chance that their diaphragms are moving in opposing directions and the variations in voltage being captured to represent the original changes in SPL in the vicinity of the microphone are potentially 180 degrees out of polarity with one another. When these signals are then played back via speakers or headphones we would hear the audible cancellation of certain frequencies. This destructive interference pertains to the phase relationships of the summed audio signals. Flipping the polarity is one way of managing and improving such audible artefacts.

One of the best drum sounds I have ever achieved came about recently using very few microphones, especially in comparison to some of my previous recordings. It all depends on what and who you arc recording. Once again, though, you have to ask yourself about the options you have and the choices you may need to take in terms of being able to manipulate the sound of the drums in post-production.

When recording a jazz trio, for example, a technique similar to the Glyn Johns technique, possibly with additional microphones on the snare (top

Using multiple microphones on a given source can be problematic in terms of phase coherence and it can be viewed as unnecessary. However, if you have the microphones and inputs but are not able to parallel a signal at the recording stage in order to process one signal and keep another clean, then using another microphone placed coincident to the other microphone can be very useful. By using two different microphones as here, with an AKG C451 B pencil condenser utilised alongside a Shure SM57 dynamic microphone (both cardioid), you can attain different tones and transient information as the microphones have different frequency and transients responses, respectively. Here the snare is also being captured by placing a third microphone underneath the snare drum, placed close to and facing the snare, although in this example the microphone is slightly off axis from the snare.

and bottom) for any extra performance detail like brushwork, would be ample.

You could also use a basic time of arrival stereo technique such as AB120 set up as overheads, with each microphone positioned 120cm apart from one another at an equal distance from the snare above the whole kit.

You can either opt to use traditional omnidirectional polar response patterns or try experimenting with directional polar patterns, such as cardioid, angling the microphones so that they face the kit with the snare and kick at the centre of an invisible line, straight above the kit or diagonally through the kick and snare. In the latter case,

place the microphones either side of the left and right line and then, when you pan, the kick and snare should still ideally be within the centre of the stereo image. You should also again consider perspective and whether it is left and right from the drummer's perspective or from the audience.

You may again wish to use additional microphones to capture the bass drum and snare to reinforce the overall back beat in the mix. It also helps with mono compatibility as there are issues when folding time of arrival stereo into mono, even when you have measured an equal distance from a centre point of the kit to either spaced microphone.

A sub microphone created from an old speaker. A moving coil microphone can be useful in capturing very low, sub frequencies and can really help to add body and weight to a recording, if subtly balanced and blended with other microphones used to capture various tones and performance articulations of the kick drum. Not all speakers, however, are ideal. Here an old speaker from Yamaha's NS10 series is being used as it has a decent 'free-air resonance', which is impacted by the moving mass of the parts, such as the weight of the cone and voice coil.

A Soundelux U195 large diaphragm condenser microphone has been placed alongside the sub microphone about 30cm away from the front skin of the drum to allow a more balanced tone to be captured in terms of the drum resonating as a whole and sound propagation within the space. Since this microphone is cardiod, and so directional, it may be worth comparing it with a large diaphragm condenser microphone set to an omni pattern to attain a flatter response. The microphone used here will capture more spill from the other drums, but overall it is about balancing the various microphones in order to attain the best sound from the drum kit as a whole.

The third microphone being used here is an Electro-Voice RE320 dynamic microphone, which is able to cope with very high SPLs. It has been placed inside the kick drum to capture more of the attack of the bass drum when the beater hits the skin. Because it captures less spill from other drums, when placed inside the drum it can be easily paralleled and processed both spectrally and dynamically to enhance the drum sound within the listening soundstage without overly exaggerating or hyping other unwanted elements of the drum kit within the mix.

Intensity (coincident or level difference) stereo techniques, such as Blumlein, MS, XY90, XY110 or any other variation, with or without additional microphones for reinforcement and control, all sound great and produce interesting results used above the drum kit as overheads, placed in front of the drums, or even behind the drummer's head.

You will find that it is worth playing around with any number of equivalence (mixed/near-coincident) stereo techniques such as ORTF, EBS, DIN, NOS and RAI. The sounds captured are generally spread well across the virtual image (SRA) and in a decent live room the time and level variations used to localise the sound can come across as more natural and less hyped. On that

On the left an AKG C451 B pencil condenser with a cardioid polar response pattern has been placed under the hi-hats and positioned slightly off axis. With phase coherence being a consideration here, you can AB test the sound in relation with the other microphones summed together in a mix by flipping the polarity button.

The large diaphragm Sony C-48 condenser microphone on the right is being used to capture the hi-hats. The microphone has been set to cardioid and tilted off axis to attain a desirable sound. This, of course, is very subjective and the 'desired' sound is related to personal taste, the functionality of what can be achieved with the recorded sound during post-production and, as always, what works best with the production brief. The microphone is here placed about 20cm above the hats and angled around 35 degrees off axis, facing away from the kit.

note it is fun to place a binaural dummy head behind the drummer's head when recording or to use baffled stereo. If the drummer spreads out how the kit is played and makes choreographed

Measuring the distance between the snare and a spaced pair

If you do not have a measuring tape, you can use a simple XLR or any other cable you have to hand that's long enough to measure the distance between the chosen focused centre point and the two spaced microphones.

movements, such recordings can make the listening soundstage sound even less static over headphones and create space and movement that can be used in a very creative manner.

However, it may be that the style of music you are recording, or the type of drum pattern being performed, requires the use of more microphones. Often, for example, with a good jazz trio or ensemble you will find that the job of a recording engineer is one of a sonic photographer and it's all about finding a great sounding room in terms of the acoustics and reverberation characteristic. Less can be more in terms of the microphones, and if the musicians are very dynamic then the recording engineers' job is mostly about the placement

In essence if you think you may need to process or manipulate a particular part of the drum kit during the mix and for production purposes, or if that part of the sound needs to be emphasised, then it may well be worth assigning a specific microphone or microphones to record that individual part of the kit or percussion instrument.

If you use only one microphone to capture the sound of a drum kit and performance as a whole and add delay, for example, then this would be applied to the whole kit. If you only want to add delay to the odd snare, however, it would be prudent to place a microphone on the snare.

Close microphone technique when recording a drum kit could be considered as the practice of when the recording engineer chooses to capture

A Shure SM7B dynamic microphone has been placed about 6cm from the snare drum with the microphone angled so that it is directly on axis, facing the top of the snare drum. Underneath a Shure SM57 dynamic microphone is being used to capture the snare's resonant head and snare. This microphone has been placed facing upwards and directly in line with the microphone placed above the snare.

of microphones, and balancing the signals you capture at source.

On the other hand, it may well be that the producer instructs an engineer to use both close microphone and ambient microphone techniques in order to provide them with more control in terms of how each drum will be balanced, placed and processed within the listening soundstage.

An example could be a performance where the drummer uses lots of toms and the production may benefit from specific spectral, spatial and/ or dynamic processing to enhance, emphasise and possibly exaggerate the sound. Here it would make sense to use a microphone to capture each drum by placing them closer to the source.

From this view you can get a better idea of the distance and positioning of the Shure SM7B near the top of the snare and the Sennheiser MD 421 dynamic microphone placed close to the rack tom, again angled to face the centre of the drum.

Additional tips for recording drums

Take the time to play with the tuning of a kick drum that has not been dampened. If you try to match the fundamental frequency with the room, or more specifically match the frequency of a standing wave, then the room becomes a natural amplifier. It is also interesting to put a second bass drum, if available, in front of the main one you have chosen to record. This can add extra resonance, body and depth in a more reverberant environment.

If you want to go further with the one microphone technique placed over the shoulder, described earlier, place a microphone directly opposite but nearer to the floor facing upwards towards the shoulder microphone. If you again picture an invisible diagonal line running through the centre of the kick and snare drum, with any other tom or cymbal either side of the line, then the floor microphone and shoulder microphone are facing opposite from one another either side of the imaginary line.

When placing a microphone outside of a bass (kick) drum for the first time, if the drum has a skin on the front, while protecting your ears, get the drummer to play the kick drum and put your hand in front of the skin or sound hole on the skin, positioning the microphone at the point where you no longer feel the air moving.

When it comes to placing a microphone close to a drum, a good starting point is to make sure you are not going to impede the player in any way as this can impact their performance. Try to place the microphone about 5cm away from the skin, just outside the rim of the drum, and point the microphone towards the centre of the drum. You will find that simply moving a directional microphone off axis by varying degrees can really alter the tone.

Do not rush into changing microphones if you are unhappy with the sound. Instead, spend some time adjusting the axis of the microphone. This is why starting with a directional microphone, such as one with a cardioid polar response pattern, in a placement where the microphone faces the centre of the drum or cymbal, is a good starting point as you can then decide whether to move the microphone +45 degrees or −45 degrees, that is upwards or downwards. Any movement can impact the amount of spill you attain, but over time balancing sounds to achieve a desirable overall tone becomes almost second nature.

Trust your ears and experiment.

The proximity effect, sometimes referred to as 'bass tip-up', can be used creatively. In essence a microphone utilising a directional polar response pattern, such as figure of eight, cardioid or hyper-cardioid, is more sensitive to low frequency, and such low frequency distortions and an increase in bass can be used to a recording engineer's advantage. This is very noticeable when using bidirectional figure of eight polar response patterns. Try experimenting with different patterns when placing a microphone in front of a kick (bass) drum.

When it comes to placing microphones above the kit, at the sides of the kit or anywhere else in the room to capture the overall sound of the drums as a whole instrument (including any cymbals being used), experiment with using different polar patterns. Traditionally time of arrival stereo techniques are set up with two microphones set in an omnidirectional pattern, but you can switch to using cardioid or figure of eight, for example.

Indeed, using microphones with directional patterns can yield really interesting results if the microphones are placed at varied angles off axis to a given sound source. A widely spaced pair of ribbons or condensers set to a figure of eight pattern either side of a drum kit, with the null points of the microphones' polar response patterns facing either side of the kit, captures some interesting detail in terms of width and tone.

If you find yourself working with a proficient and dynamic drummer who can balance themselves and the sound of the drum kit as a whole while performing, then I often find that basic techniques such as the Glyn Johns will benefit from the microphone channels being bussed together into one subgroup. The subgroup can then be subtly fed into compressors set up to grab the transients in a slower, smoother musical manner to add tone and cohesion. LA2A opto compressors, a Fairchild tube compressor or a pulse width modulation compressor like the PYE are fun to play with.

individually the sound of a specific drum by placing a microphone directly on it or any individual part of the kit, including cymbals. How close you position the microphone is up to you: too close and the proximity effect becomes more of a consideration and too far away and you will ultimately attain less separation.

You can also choose to use multiple microphones placed close to any of the drums in order to capture different tones or if you have limitations in being able to duplicate or 'parallel' a signal.

It may well be the case that you want to keep one signal clean while simultaneously processing the same sound being captured by feeding it through a different signal chain. Larger studios have patch bays that allow the engineer to parallel signals in this manner. You can of course easily duplicate a recorded signal in a DAW at a later date, but using an additional microphone, if you have one, and the inputs can yield some great results in more ways than one.

FOLDBACK

Taking the time to get a decent foldback mix really helps. It is not just a case of balance (level and spectral) and what the performer wants to hear in their headphones.

Though it is hugely important, any sort of delay can be very off-putting for a player and no two people hear the same mix.

Latency in a modern digital recording system can cause delay. In essence, every time the drummer hits a drum they may then hear its sound played back late in their headphones. I have been in a situation where the buffer size has been turned down to its lowest setting and all plugins removed. Although I could not hear any delay, the recording artist could.

It goes to say that it is not worth getting into an argument before a session, as performance can be driven by the overall mood of a session. In regards to the mood of a given session, aesthetics play a role. Paul Winter-Hart, who has drummed on many a session over the years and is a member of the band Kula Shaker, has

always played with the lighting in the live room where his drums have been set up. There will be more about what Paul has to say about recording drums below.

All I would say at this juncture is that, regardless of whether, like Paul, a drummer wants to hear only a kick drum in his headphones or prefers a more full-on, detailed foldback mix, including many of the various drums that make up a standard five-piece kit, getting the mix right in the player's cans is vital. More elaborate foldback mixes with multiple elements being sent to the performer can be highly influential, so a recording engineer is not just capturing a sound.

Great sounding drums enhanced by choosing particular microphones, tried and tested placement and appropriate gain staging with preamps that add harmonic colour and tone, in line with further spectral and dynamic processing, can help to really exaggerate the size and resonance of a drum.

This, alongside interesting acoustics, can really impact the creative aspect of tracking when sent to a player's headphones and inspire the performer to play in a manner that takes the performance energy, dynamics and production's aesthetic in a new direction.

If you have the opportunity to provide direct monitoring to the performer before the A/D stage within the modern recording chain, then this is preferable and can really help when it comes to capturing a great performance in terms of groove, syncopation, and performance articulations.

This is one of the many bonuses when working with analogue mixing consoles that have been wired in a practical and ultimately flexible manner.

Even though many recording engineers choose to record with multiple microphones in order to give themselves and their colleagues a series of options to capture and manipulate the listening soundstage, it is not necessary to send all the captured signals back to the drummer's headphones.

Paul Winter-Hart, for example, likes only a little bit of the bass drum in his headphones and foldback mix when recording. This is even when I am recording with multiple microphones to capture various parts of the drum kit, including up to three microphones on the kick, and could offer him a more nuanced, balanced blend of sounds that have often been processed via hardware 'on the way in', so to speak. Even then he asks for just the kick to be bussed directly out of the desk into his cans, alongside some of the click track and a previously agreed mix of the elements in the backing track he is wanting to play along to, such as vocals or bass.

In contrast, I always like to have at least kick and snare in my cans, and some drummers I have worked with, though rarely, ask for the overheads. A multitude of different combinations can be achieved, but I have rarely come across performers asking for room microphones placed at a distance, in effect ambient microphones, to be added to their foldback mix, because in some circumstances they can find this very distracting and it can lead to issues with timing. Nonetheless, if the recording engineer spends some time processing incoming signals to sound larger than life, for example by compression or using reverb, such exaggerated sounds can be sent to a foldback mix in order to inspire and influence how the drummer performs.

Often in such circumstances an engineer will parallel channels – think of this as duplicating if it's easier to picture – so that they can capture a clean and processed signal simultaneously. This is helpful for many reasons, some of which, such as creative re-amping, will be discussed in Chapter 7.

One thing to be aware of, however, is that when it comes to certain types of processing and recording drums an engineer may look towards asking the drummer to approach playing in a different manner. An example of this is when dynamic processing, namely compression, is introduced to the signal chain in order to exaggerate a given sound. In this situation a kick and snare can be processed alongside appropriate amplification to create a larger than life, incredibly powerful drum sound within the listening soundstage, effectively altering the envelope of the given sounds. In such circumstances the headphones mix provided by the engineer can inspire the drummer and be conducive to creative and artistic decision-making in terms of a performance. It may be best, however, to ask the drummer just to play the kick and snare pattern and overdub any cymbal crashes, which can sound very harsh and overbearing with excessive dynamic processing.

6

GUITARS, PIANO AND ENSEMBLE RECORDING

Unlike recording a full drum kit, when it comes to recording an acoustic guitar, a cello, viola or violin, for example, there is a logistical freedom that can be used to a recording engineer's advantage. A guitar, for example, is portable and you can therefore move the player into a variety of spaces. Tiled bathrooms can be very reflective and the room acoustics can brighten and energise your recording.

An instrument such as a fairly portable acoustic guitar also does not generate the same sound pressure levels as a drum kit hit with sticks when aiming for a specific heavy-hitting performance and its subsequent tone and production aesthetic. You do not necessarily have to record in a specific location or fancy studio live room. Indeed, as I mentioned earlier in the Preface, I once captured one of my favourite recorded performances in the living room of an old flat. Granted I had high ceilings that helped craft a pleasing reverberation characteristic, and very accommodating neighbours, but nevertheless certain instruments can be recorded very well in a variety of spaces.

It is often beneficial to record drums in larger treated spaces such as purpose-built studio live rooms, not just to reduce the risk of your neighbours making a complaint, but also because of the nature and, more specifically, the wavelengths of the frequencies generated by drums and the chance for standing waves and room modes to become an issue in an untreated room. This is not another chapter on drum recording, but what I am alluding to is that where we chose to record

Calculating wavelengths

In order to calculate the wavelength of a particular frequency, take the speed of sound, which is stated in the *Master Handbook of Acoustics* (*see* Chapter 1) as a value of 344m/sec, and divide it by the frequency. Let's say the lowest string and note on a guitar, an 'E', is 83Hz (or a near variation), then 344 divided by 83 equals 4.14. So the wavelength is 4.14m. By comparison, a five-string bass with the additional low 'B' string can go down as low as 31Hz and yield a wavelength of 11m. The latter example may be more problematic in terms of standing waves, peaks and nodes when setting up a bass amp and wanting to play at high SPLs in an average smaller untreated room at home. You can, of course, turn a bass amplifier down, but it's not so easy with acoustic drums, especially if you do not want to compromise the performance.

can have an impact on the sound and how our performers play. Ultimately this affects the recording and production aesthetic.

As well as easily being able to move an acoustic guitar and the player into different spaces, setting up microphones to capture such an instrument can really help you improve and hone your skills as a recording engineer.

In this instance you can sit and listen, ideally via speakers in a separate control room, in the same room with some isolation or via headphones

Blumlein technique configured using two AKG C414 microphones set to bidirectional figure of eight polar response patterns and placed at 90 degrees from one another.

to how the sound of the instrument changes in terms of the tone captured, how the localisation of the guitar and stereo image alters if you are using stereo recording techniques, simply by asking the musician to move around. This is very hard with a piano, with or without wheels (not to mention tuning issues that might arise moving a piano), or with a drum kit with multiple microphones set up.

RECORDING ACOUSTIC GUITAR

There is something very pleasing and natural sounding about capturing acoustic string instruments using the Blumlein technique. I have always found that if I am recording more than one person playing acoustic guitar, for example,

having the musicians face one another at opposing sides of such a stereo configuration yields great results.

You can sit in a control room or, if on location, monitor via headphones and instruct the players to move around until you find a pleasing balance in terms of placement, image and balance, both in terms of level and spectrally.

Because the Blumlein technique uses two figure of eight polar response patterns, when you place musicians such as two guitarists facing one another it is nearly akin to using two separate XY90 configurations (albeit an XY90 level difference technique typically combines two cardioid polar response patterns). The point is that if both musicians are placed so that the chosen reference point of their guitar is facing the centre of the Blumlein configuration, then through using just the one technique and some choice placement you can get an evenly spread image with good localisation cues over the full breadth of the two speakers.

Recording to two separate mono channels, rather than one stereo channel, in your chosen DAW allows you to manipulate the recorded image. Essentially, if you attenuate or boost one of the faders away from its relative level at the time of recording then you are impacting the level differences initially captured via the two coincident microphone diaphragms, and it is the differences in these levels that help us to localise a given sound source at the reproduction or monitoring stage.

Included here is a series of photos showing various spaced pairs and dual mono microphone

Guitar tuning consistency

As with other instruments, it is important that an acoustic guitar is in good working order and set up correctly. For recordings to be consistent when tracking multiple takes of the same part or overdubbing, it is always a good idea to use the same tuner as a reference point and, if possible, tune between the takes being recorded.

Variation of the XY coincident technique. The angle between the microphones, placed as close together as possible without touching, is 100 degrees, so we could refer to the configuration as XY100. This could be considered unorthodox as engineers usually opt for XY90, XY120 and so on, but it is all about how it sounds ultimately. The SRA captured a virtual image that spread the guitar over the speakers in a manner suitable for the production in question.

DIN equivalence/near-coincident mixed stereo technique in a configuration using two AKG C451 B pencil condensers with a cardioid polar response pattern. The microphones are set at an angle of 90 degrees with 20cm between them.

ORTF equivalence/near-coincident mixed stereo technique, also using two AKG C451 B microphones. This time there is a 17cm distance and 110-degree angle between the microphones. The centre of the configuration is facing the soundhole in this instance, but at a distance that is not problematic in terms of distortion. Once again I would recommend moving the musician around until you find a sound you are happy with.

An acoustic guitar being recorded via two pencil condensers with cardioid polar response patterns. The XY90 coincident, intensity level difference stereo configuration is placed off axis from the sound source.

Recording acoustic guitar and vocals at the same time

When recording acouistic guitar try using XY90 or XY110 configurations. In the example shown on page 87 you can see that the point where the microphones meet, forming something like the tip of an arrow, is tilting upwards. Here you are in effect placing the stereo recording technique as a whole off axis in terms of the sound source and the most direct path from the sound source to the most sensitive part of the microphones' diaphragms.

Playing around with the positioning of the microphones in terms of how many degrees they are off axis can yield very pleasing results. Here the microphones are 45 degrees off axis.

By elevating the position of the microphones and changing the angle, you can also experiment with capturing more of a phase-cohesive performance than when using two separate microphones if the artist wishes to sing and play at the same time. Such cohesion, to be discussed further in Chapter 8, really helps in post-production when looking at spectral and dynamic processing.

A pair of AKG C414 condensers set to pick up via an omni polar response pattern being used to configure a basic AB60 time of arrival stereo technique or 'spaced pair'.

placements being used to capture an acoustic guitar. From a purely technical perspective a conscientious engineer would spend time measuring distances between microphones and looking at such considerations as that the microphones are equidistant from a given reference point of the sound source being recorded. With an acoustic guitar this reference point can be wherever produces the best results. In part this is again related to the quality of the instrument and the room you are recording in.

A good starting point might be around the twelfth or thirteenth fret and with a wider AB configuration of around 60cm or more placed 60cm or so away from the instrument, using the sound hole as your point of reference. Getting too close to the sound hole can be problematic as low frequency builds up and causes a bottleneck at this specific area of the instrument. Like all acoustic instruments, and more specifically the concept of acoustic resonance, you will get a more natural and balanced overall tone if you position the microphone(s) further away, although this may well depend upon the quality of the room acoustics. In a well-treated live room with controlled acoustic energy you can move your microphones a metre or so away and still get a well-defined sound in the low end of the frequency spectrum, while retaining intelligibility and clarity in the mid-range.

A spaced pair, time of arrival stereo configuration that utilises two condenser microphones set to an omnipolar response pattern can capture and reproduce spatial cues that, with thought and considered placement, recreate a decent representation of the reverberant sound within a given room when played back over speakers or headphones.

A variation of a spaced pair, time of arrival stereo technique using two large diaphragm AKG C414 microphones (experiment with using different polar response patterns, though such a technique traditionally uses omni patterns).

This is why I often set up a wider AB120 configuration in conjunction with other stereo techniques or arrays placed closer to a given acoustic instrument. The latter is to capture detail, while the AB120 is used to capture the ambience of the room.

Unfortunately we don't all have access to well-treated spaces to record, or for that matter the equipment that many studios provide to make our lives easier, including something as simple as a stereo bar. This is an attachment for a microphone stand that allows the user to mount two or more microphones. Not only does this save space and time, but often they come with well-labelled spacings and markings to help identify the angles and measure the distances between the microphones.

I raise this issue having earlier alluded to the vital importance of the diligent attention to detail that any engineer must observe as a prerequisite of specialist recordings – and yet many of my best recordings of acoustic guitar have come by breaking away from conventions and exploring variations of well-known and respected techniques.

For one, try switching to using alternative polar response patterns such as cardioid or hyper cardioid when using a spaced pair, time of arrival stereo technique. Alternatively, do not treat the two microphones as part of a configuration and instead use them as two individual mono microphones to capture a certain part and tone of the instrument. In that arrangement you do not need to be concerned about using two microphones of the same type or model as tonal balance will be achieved by blending the sounds via balancing levels and panning.

The results attained by the various techniques depicted in this series differ in how wide the instrument sounds over the reproduction system and in tonal balance. One way is position the microphones in a diagonal manner closer to the instrument. Place a condenser microphone set to an omni polar response pattern about 50cm away from the instrument near to the larger side of the body, to the right of the bridge (from the guitarist's perspective). By placing the microphone here you can capture plenty of low end detail and resonance, but the tone is more balanced so you find yourself using less corrective or, if you prefer, subtractive EQ.

Diagonally placed large diaphragm c414 condenser microphones. The one to the left is set to an omni polar response pattern and placed at a the distance you feel obtains a suitable tonal balance, in terms of low end body and definition emanating from the instrument. The one to the right is set to a cardioid polar response pattern and placed at different angles in relation to sensitivity and the axis of the microphone to attain a tone that complements the overall tonal balance when blended with the left microphone.

The other condenser is set to cardioid to capture more of the directional frequencies (ray energy, as opposed to low end wave energy below 100Hz) emanating from that part of the body and neck. In this instance the sound hole, twelfth, thirteenth or indeed any fret are not being used as a reference point, so there is no need to work out a placement for the microphones that is equidistant from a given point.

The microphone can be angled until you feel that the off-axis attenuation of lower frequencies complements the overall tonal balance when blended and balanced with the other microphone. The second microphone is positioned slightly closer to the instrument, around 30cm away. As a variation of this technique, the second microphone can be moved further away to capture more of the room sound.

Precisely how you place, balance and blend the sounds captured via panning and adjusting the faders to create an overall tone with which you are happy is down to you. Though keeping an eye on a correlation meter can be helpful, once again use your ears. How does it sound to you?

The MS technique is also suited to recording an acoustic guitar. In this instance the MID microphone, set to a cardioid polar response pattern, is facing the thirteenth fret and is positioned

A variation of the diagonally placed microphones, where the microphones are placed further away to capture more of the room sound.

Another variation using two large diaphragm condensers, this time the microphone to the left is placed more towards the side of the guitar's body, and the second microphone, again set to an omni polar pattern, is placed further away from the neck in order to capture more of the room sound.

around 1m away from the guitar. Again, the technique is ideal when mono compatibility is a concern, but when this configuration is used in a fairly large space, having the option to alter the width and centre image within the subsequent mix of the recording gives a sense of flexibility. It may well be that you want a more intimate, close and upfront sound in your production with the added option to open up the sound when required during the mix.

The overall stereo image of a guitar captured in this way is not usually overly hyped and out of proportion. This is good in that you can easily work with mismatched microphones and experiment to achieve some varied and interesting results, as long as a bidirectional microphone is angled at 90 degrees away from the centre of the soundstage or chosen point of focus when recording the instrument. If on the other hand you are using MS to record a larger ensemble, then it is best to use similar microphones in terms of operating principle and model because otherwise the tonal balance can be audibly impacted when you are required to capture a wider soundstage.

The MS technique can also be employed, using a microphone with a cardioid polar response pattern positioned about 1m away from the guitar, facing the 13th fret.

Earlier I admitted to using too many microphones when I first started out as an engineer. I still stand by the 'less really can be more' perspective, but there are occasions where mixing up techniques has helped me to capture some really great sounding recordings.

At the very least I have been able to record and walk away with options to control the listening soundstage during the mix.

The XY90 technique can be used to capture the overall tone and stereo image of a guitar. The tip or point where the microphones meet faces the sound hole and is placed about 60cm away. A large diaphragm condenser set to cardioid polar response pattern is placed about 80cm from the main body of the guitar (again to the right of the bridge from the guitarist's perspective). This additional microphone can be used to add additional detail to the overall sound and can be moved closer

Multiple microphones (from left to right: Brauner Phantom V, Blue Baby Bottle condenser and AKG C451 B pencil condenser) being used to capture various tones and performance articulations.

Using the XY90 technique, and an additional, single microphone (large diaphragm condenser in this example) to capture the overall stereo image of the guitar and to reinforce, or add more body to the sound.

if required, although this will increase how much low end is captured.

If all stages of the signal chain have a good signal to noise ratio and the room acoustics are suitable, then additional gain or some appropriate upward compression that grabs the transients in a musical manner to suit the style of the performance, can really help alter the perceived size and tonal balance of the instrument within the listening soundstage and mix.

A similar approach can be employed by positioning the stereo configuration behind the two microphones being used to focus on the resonance from the main body of the guitar and additional detail emanating from the upper bout and neck.

RECORDING ELECTRIC GUITAR AND BASS

Like any of the instruments we have discussed, it could be argued that ultimately the most important factor when using one or more microphones to record an instrument is how it sounds and not how they look in terms of where they are being placed. It is easy to get embroiled in very technical and precise detail if you are concerned about specialised formats, phase coherence and down mixing, for example from stereo to mono.

When you are not constrained or tied to such considerations it is about having a vision from the outset regarding what sort of sound you want to capture and how it will sit within the listening soundstage. How big should the sound be, should it be in the forefront and narrow, in the background and wide or vice versa, or anywhere in-between?

Alongside listening to lots of records and choosing a reference, it is once again about getting out and recording. When it comes to using amplifiers and the various tones that can be crafted, however, there are situations when it may be necessary to really crank up the gain (if not quite to *This Is Spinal Tap*'s 'up to eleven') and work with very high SPLs. For this you often need a decent room to work with. Of course, finding a room with an interesting reverberation characteristic can sometimes yield such pleasing results that a whole new production aesthetic is born, and in turn this can lead the project in a new direction.

When the room does not sound great, however, or if you just want a more upfront and less roomy sound, you may opt to place your microphone or microphones close to the amp.

You can, of course, opt for placing microphones further away if you think the sound of the room is

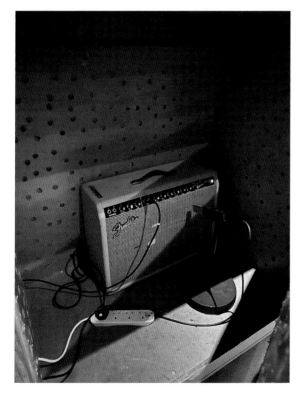

Here the guitar amp is housed in an isolation booth and a Sennheiser MD 441 dynamic microphone, which can cope with very high SPLs, has been positioned on axis and to the right of the speaker within the Fender 65 deluxe.

An Ampeg B-15 Portaflex being captured by a large diaphragm AKG C414 set to an omnipolar response pattern with attenuation being applied via a pad on the microphone. The amp was not being cranked and the microphone coped well with fairly high SPLs. Here the microphone is placed fairly central in relation to the speaker at about 18cm away.

The Orange amp is being captured by a Shure SM7B, placed on axis right against the grill, and a Coles 4038 ribbon microphone placed on axis about 2.5cm away.

A Marshall stack and a vintage Yamaha PE-200 amp being captured (from left to right) by a Shure SM7B dynamic, a Sennheiser MD 421 dynamic, a Bock Audio 195 condenser and a Coles 4038 ribbon.

workable or adds some much-needed depth to the listening soundstage. Often engineers will use a combination of microphone types and placement in order to build a wall of sound and provide options for when it comes to mixing. When we return to the idea of a mix being like telling a story, then a change in energy throughout a mix can help create emphasis. Recording plays a huge part in capturing this energy in the first instance. Techniques to create such changes may include simply muting channels until needed. Having options also gives the recording and mix engineer options as to where other elements can sit and blend in the listening soundstage, and mix in terms of the frequency spectrum and placement between the speakers (if working in stereo or beyond).

In scenarios when multiple amps are being used you can consider a stereo configuration such as MS or other intensity stereo techniques. These can be easily folded down to mono but can be used in stereo to add width to the recording and capture the ambience of the room.

DIRECT INJECT (DI) BOXES

DI boxes were developed and became widely used in response to the needs of changing technology and the widespread use of electrical instruments in the 1960s. At its very basic a DI box can be used to rectify issues pertaining to impedance by helping to match the signal level between an instrument and a preamp.

Recording guitar amplifiers

Try raising the amp off from the floor by placing it on a stand, some crates, another amp or anything that can carry its weight. This can alter both the tone and projection of the sound. When an amp is on the floor there can be a boost in low frequencies, which could work to your advantage depending on what you are trying to obtain, but in some instances it may colour the sound unfavourably and impact how the sound behaves in terms of reflections, diffracting, refractions and so on.

Depending on the floor surface you can sometimes obtain a very interesting sound by positioning a directional microphone at floor level a metre or so away from an amp placed on the floor or raised up, although when the former it can be especially noticeable if the floor material is very reflective or sometimes acts as a resonator.

Some amplifiers are open at the back and positioning a microphone here to face the rear of the speaker can obtain some very pleasing and usable tones. Just remember to flip the polarity on your preamp if the microphone in question is facing another one placed to face the front of the speaker.

A DI box takes an unbalanced, high impedance signal, such as one coming from the pickup of an electric guitar or bass, and converts the output signal into a balanced, low impedance signal. Depending on the transformers used to help convert the signal and how they are wound, they can also help reduce noise, specifically ground loops and hum. DI boxes often come with

A splitter box being used alongside the 'thru' of a DI so that the signal outputted from the guitar can be sent to more than one amp. In this instance there is a bass cab with an Ashdown Little Bastard 30 and a Laney Cub 12. The latter is being captured via a Shure SM57 and the former via an SM7B and an sE Electronics X1D. There are other ways to achieve the effect of using multiple amps simultaneously, but in this scenario the guitarist wanted two independent sounds to be summed together. It was important that the two amps were not chained together and both gain and level could be tweaked individually. In this particular session using different amps and microphones was a great way to layer the sounds in a manner that complemented the overall spectral balance.

a ground lift, which can also help with ground loops.

DI boxes can be either passive and active. The difference is that active DI boxes use a preamp to help boost the lower output of certain instruments, such as those that may be using only single coil pickups.

DI BOXES IN USE

If you have a band who wish to track live together to capture that all-important natural feel of a performance, it can be difficult if you do not have separate live rooms to work in or access to isolation cabinets. Using an amp in the same room as drums, for example, can be especially

A slightly different configuration being used to add a different tone to the various layers of guitars. An Orange amp and cab is being captured via a Coles 4038 ribbon microphone and an SM7B dynamic. Here XY110 (coincident) intensity/level difference stereo is being utilised to capture the ambience, the sound of the amp in the room. This type of stereo configuration, placed 2.5m away from the amp, was used because the SRA worked well on this occasion and offered better phase coherence and mono compatibility when down mixed and summed with the microphones placed close to the amp.

problematic if you need to minimise spill while wanting to craft a specific production aesthetic during post and where maximising separation is a big consideration.

In this scenario a DI box is really useful because the engineer can capture the sound of a bass or guitar, amplify and then bus back (foldback) out to the musician's headphones. The recorded signals can then be re-amped at a later stage (see Chapter 7).

This is far from ideal for many guitarists, however, as they often work with the tone of the amps to help craft a performance. Sounding right, feeling right … it's all connected. There are decent amp emulators that come in the form of a pedal or hardware unit that can work in line with a DI that can negate the need for a speaker, but again this is not always the best solution.

I would suggest that even when you are able to access a studio with multiple live rooms to house amps in something similar to isolation cabinets, it is still good practice to incorporate a DI box alongside the amp or amps of your choice.

Not only do some DI boxes add tone, but if you use the 'thru' function you can capture the unprocessed, clean sound (clean as in post pickups, but before the guitar amplifier stage) while paralleling the signal into an amp that can then be recorded by a microphone or multiple microphones. This in effect gives you the best of both worlds, as now if there are any issues with the amp sound at the time of recording, you can re-amp the DI sound at any later stage.

DI boxes are used for all sorts of instruments and tools in the studio, for example when a musician wants to use hardware synthesisers, drum machines and samplers.

There are even occasions when an artist may want to set up their own workspace and use a laptop, DAW and outboard alongside various other musicians to perform live. In this instance they may have an audio interface with multiple outputs and require multiple DI boxes (mono, stereo or both).

If the artist then wants to use the timeline in their DAW as the master clock for the session so they can control any tempo or time signature changes,

Bass guitar being recorded via a DI box and two microphones. In this scenario the recording engineer is capturing three channels. The DI box is providing a direct, clean tone to the recording device, while simultaneously being sent/paralleled, via the 'thru' output, into a pedal board and then via the pedal board into an Ashdown Little Bastard amp. This then feeds onto the speaker cab, where a Shure SM7B and an sE Electronics X1D microphone are being utilised to capture the tone emanating from the cab.

then even more considerations come into play, not least separating the click track so it can be bussed out via an individual channel to the other musicians' headphone mix.

A Radial passive stereo DI box. Such a device may be ideal for when an artist wants to interface their whole workspace with your recording set-up.

THE BASICS OF RECORDING AN ENSEMBLE

Since this book's target audience is hobbyists and semi-professionals possibly wishing to brush up on the basics and look towards developing ideas they may wish to research further, it may seem that the photo of an orchestra being recorded may seem a little over the top. The same could be said of many of the photos included here if you take a literal view of the environment, scenario and equipment shown as indicating how you need to progress as a recording engineer. This really is not the case and I would always suggest that you focus on the concept being discussed and, perhaps more pertinently, how you can apply such practice as you choose based on what you have access to.

With this in mind, being realistic and working with what we have available, I am always

A Decca tree being used as the main array when recording an orchestra in order to capture the whole soundstage.

surprised how rarely people try to approach the custodian of a particular space with interesting acoustics, such as a church or hall. Maybe I have been lucky, but I have always found people to be very accommodating if your request is timely and, again, realistic.

When it comes to recording a group of musicians or 'ensemble', the focus is on capturing that ever important performance (timing, phrasing, articulation and so on). Generally editing during post-production can be difficult for many reasons, not least because often when capturing a live performance at a concert with an audience, for example, the musicians and recording engineer get only one chance to capture the performance – unless you record rehearsals without the audience and dub in some ambience or the, thankfully, extremely

rare occurrence when a performance has to be stopped mid-flow in front of an audience before starting again.

Whether you are looking at capturing a one-off performance or are able to record multiple takes, finding a suitable environment is paramount, at least from the recording engineer's perspective. I appreciate I have said this about every situation, but on this occasion it is not just the acoustics but the logistics of potentially working with larger numbers of musicians.

Whether a brass ensemble, string quartet, quintet, choir or full-size orchestra, you can capture an excellent recording via any number of stereo techniques, though many practitioners claim to have obtained great results by using equivalence stereo configurations such

An outrigger placed at the edge of the stage can be seen to the right of the Decca tree in the distance. In the foreground a Beyerdynamic M160 ribbon microphone with a hyper-cardioid polar response pattern is being used as a spot microphone.

A Decca Tree using three Neumann U 87 condenser microphones set to omnidirectional polar response patterns has been placed behind the conductor at the centre of the intended soundstage to be recorded. The U 87s on a microphone stand specially adapted for a Decca Tree configuration have been tilted to alter the depth perception of the recording, and because ultimately it sounded better.

as ORTF. Although the technique is not without its critics, using a Decca Tree, which utilises three microphones set to omnidirectional polar response patterns as the main array in order to capture the whole soundstage, can give excellent results.

The addition of a third microphone in the 1950s has been credited in part to the angular distortion that occurred in early stereophonic recordings captured via a widely spaced configuration. The idea was that by adding a third microphone the issue of an apparent hole in the centre of the image would be rectified when reproduced virtually over speakers.

When recording ensembles and orchestras I would, on this occasion, recommend experimenting with higher sample rates such as 88kHz or 96kHz (if possible, and if you have access to quality recording equipment and converters), especially if you are on location and the space has a noticeable reverberation characteristic.

Personally, and I stress the word 'personally', I have found that, when using higher sample rates, some of my location recordings sound more detailed and defined in the way they capture the players and the room's acoustics and, dare I say, sometimes the recordings have felt more emotive.

An additional stereo configuration being used in conjunction with the main Decca tree. In this instance two more U87s are set up in an ORTF configuration. This was to reinforce and capture further detail in regards to some of the instruments further back within the recorded soundstage. The decision was made as the reverberation times and specific character of the room at various frequencies led to a loss of clarity and intelligibility.

Many practitioners, however, argue that higher sample rates can be detrimental and are only useful for very specialist applications such as processing (for example stretching the audio to speed up or down), manipulating sound for sound design purposes, restoration work or working with spatial audio and VR. I would highly recommend reading some of the white papers on sampling theory by Dan Lavry.

Choosing an appropriate stereo configuration that yields an SRA that complements the various sound sources being recorded, both in terms of detail and placement, can be paramount if the brief is to capture a decent and fairly natural representation of the soundstage. Michael Williams cites the idea of 'angular distortion' in which, in the simplest of terms, the sound sources being captured can be distorted or skewed when attempting to visualise how they appear to be placed virtually between the speakers at the reproduction stage. In some instances the instrument or various sound sources you are capturing can appear to be bunched up between the speakers in the centre of the image, or pushed up and bunched together in the other direction, towards the speakers.

Here it is not just a matter of choosing an appropriate configuration to capture a desirable SRA for the brief, but it is where the configuration is positioned. Whether recording a brass section, strings, a choir or any number of musicians and combinations of instruments, it is good to choose a configuration or array that can be placed in an appropriate position to capture the whole soundstage. The centre point in front of a given soundstage from the audience's perspective is normally a good starting position. This could, for example, be behind the conductor or choirmaster.

Once you have placed your configuration at the centre point and listened to the SRA to see if it yields a pleasing spread from left to right over your speakers, you need to consider raising the chosen stereo configuration or multi-microphone array so it can be adjusted in a way that helps you capture the instruments and sounds with a decent sense of depth or detail from the front to the back of the soundstage.

After this point, if the soundstage is very wide and the stereo configuration or array you have chosen needs reinforcement, you can add 'outriggers' to the very left- and right-hand side, facing (if using directional pickup patterns such as cardioid) the soundstage you intend to capture. Effectively such additional microphones flank either side of the chosen array and though they are too far apart to be correlated in any manner, and therefore not considered as stereo, they can be used with a considered amount of balance and panning to enhance what the main centred stereo technique or larger array has captured.

It is also common to use 'spot' microphones closer to individual instruments or sections to help reinforce sections of a larger orchestra, a particular aspect of a performance, or highlight, rebalance and bring out a solo.

Once again it is about experimenting and putting the ideas you may have into practice. Choosing a suitable space to record in is paramount. Rooms that have too much treatment, namely absorption, tend to lack high frequency energy and detail, whereas some spaces are awash with reflections and the reverberation characteristic can be detrimental in terms of capturing the performance articulations, and any real distinguishable clarity, definition and intelligibility associated with a given sound or instrument.

Recording ensembles, whether in the studio or on location at a concert, is really about getting a great sound at the source. Though we can argue this is the case with everything we have discussed, when it comes to musicians playing together aspects such as how notes are articulated or phrased, alongside pitch and timing, become more noticeable than ever. There may be tools at the engineer's disposal that can help with some corrective aspects, normally applied after the recording, but they are limited in some respects.

Recording strings is an example that comes to mind. There are tools that work with pitch and tuning at a polyphonic level, while some can even be applied to help with timing, but in my experience they can struggle with the many other aspects associated with performance articulation and

Recording multiple instruments at various distances from a source

When recording with multiple microphones at such distances, usually when there is 4m or more between them, consider using delay and/or some tool or technique to help with time/phase alignment (*see* Chapter 8). This can sometimes help to mini-mise issues pertaining to destructive interference and phase coherence, such as image distortion and the colourisation of sound/tonal loss due to frequency cancellation. A very basic rule is that 1ms equates to around 1ft (more like 0.9ms/ft) of sound travelled (in the case of multiple micro-phones in relation to a given sound source, this is the distance between microphones). This is a very basic interpretation, however, and many practition-ers give varied examples as to how they calculate how to apply delay and time offsets between the main array used to capture a given soundstage

and a signal(s) capturing or being used to support and reinforce sections of the soundstage. When summed this can cause comb filtering and image distortion. Once again it is about being aware that such phenomena might occur. Take some meas-urements between the main array and spot micro-phones, if necessary, and then experiment with delaying by milliseconds and inverting the polar-ity of the microphones supporting the main array, including the spots and outriggers.

Ultimately you have to listen and train your ears. There are plugins and tools to help, and of course you can undertake further research into the param-eters, metrics and mathematical notation with which you need to be familiar when using more accurate equations to calculate and possibly arrive at a better outcome in terms of audible clarity.

intonation when naturalness is an integral part of the brief.

THE BASICS OF RECORDING A PIANO

I have always found recording piano, a percus-sive chordophone instrument (considered as both a string instrument and pitched percus-sion), one of the more challenging, but also more rewarding endeavours. It is often very difficult to get the sound you are looking for at first, especially when you are unfamiliar with a given model and the room acoustics where the piano is housed.

If you are hiring a studio specifically to record piano, it is often worth asking the in-house engi-neers if they have any suggestions or tips as to how they would approach the recording and how they would set about trying to attain a particular sound that fits with the production aesthetic you have in mind.

I was really lucky to have spent some time working in a studio in Liverpool that housed a beautiful-sounding Blüthner grand piano. I was able to spend time experimenting with a variety of microphones and techniques, and where to posi-tion the microphones. How an instrument sounds to our ears and how the sound of an instrument being recorded via microphones translates over speakers are two very different actualities, not least because unless specialist considerations, microphones and playback formats are taken into consideration, most recordings will not capture height cues.

So as always it is using the tools at hand, start-ing with the microphones, as colouring tools to paint a picture to our canvas, the DAW, that we feel does the production justice.

I often found that achieving such goals came via experimentation and lots of time spent recording. I would set up multiple stereo configurations along-side individual microphones placed fairly close to different parts of the piano in order to listen and see what tones I could capture.

Multiple Mono Microphone Technique: a Brauner Phantom V (upper left), a Bock Audio 195 (upper right) and a Coles 4038 (underneath the piano) being used as three independent mono microphones to capture various tones emanating from the piano. When combined and balanced the microphones capturing different tones can be summed to reproduce an overall picture of the instrument that is full-bodied, rich and defined. Such microphone techniques need not be panned.

Placing a large diaphragm condenser microphone or a dynamic (an AKG D12 was a good choice) underneath the centre of the piano facing upwards at the soundboard, for example, helped to capture some of the very low end body and weight of the instrument.

It was also interesting to place a pencil condenser or ribbon microphone over the rim at the rear of the piano facing the frame, with or without the lid being attached to the piano.

Upright pianos, like grand pianos, will change considerably in terms of the resonance and the overall tone of the instrument when you experiment by taking away various panels. Removing the bottom front panel, for example, helps to capture a more direct sound from the soundboard and strings. In the example shown here, a Coles 4038 ribbon has been tilted to face the strings facing in-between the bass and treble bridge. The top panels have been taken off to reveal the hammer rail and hammers. This can be really effective when recording treated pianos and when you want to capture some of the mechanical noise.

In the same photo three microphones are being placed independently of one another as opposed to being configured for a stereo recording. Although there are time of arrival differences, the microphones are treated as being unrelated in terms of discerning localisation cues via time and level differences. Here the room, or more specifically the reverberation characteristic, worked well in enhancing certain tones of the piano over the frequency spectrum and therefore each microphone was placed at a different distance from the piano to capture a different tone in relation to the ratio between direct and reverberant sound, although the differences were subtle. The many approaches to recording a piano, or indeed any instrument, shown in this section often require the engineer to place the microphones, then take time to listen before returning to adjust the positioning of the microphones until the necessary overall tonal balance has been achieved.

The placement of the microphones in the same example was decided after experimenting with moving the piano into the centre of the room and placing microphones to face and capture sound emanating from the rear panel and soundboard. Due to the room acoustics, it was decided that the best results were achieved by placing the piano up against the wall and by removing various panels. The two large diaphragm condensers that can be seen were not equidistant from any point of the piano and were moved individually until the sounds emanating from the piano were balanced with the sounds captured by the other microphone facing the strings. There was no array or configuration as such, just good old-fashioned balance achieved by placing the three microphones where sweet spots were found and balancing the sound they captured to attain an overall tone suited to the project.

If you get the chance to work either in a live room with controlled acoustics or with a flattering and usable reverberation characteristic, then, as is often the case with acoustic instruments, moving

Brauner Phantom V and Bock Audio 195 large diaphragm condensers, both set to a cardioid polar response pattern, are being used in a modified time of arrival stereo technique similar to an AB120 spaced pair.

Two AKG C451 B pencil condensers placed so that they are focused on a section of the piano rather than the whole range from a spectrally balanced point of view. By making use of the directional polar response pattern, different tonal changes can be captured by on- and off-axis placement to achieve the desired tone for the client and brief.

Another two microphones have been added and placed below the keyboard to face the soundboard, treble and bass strings. In this instance the two Coles 4038 ribbons are again placed in a configuration similar to a wide-spaced pair in terms of the distance and time of arrival differences being used, when the channels are panned, to help localise the sound. Since both ribbon microphones have figure of eight polar patterns, they have been tilted to face the centre point of the treble and bass strings, respectively.

the microphones further away from the piano can capture a really nice balanced and natural tone. Any of the stereo techniques we have discussed can often be utilised in a very effective manner depending on the type of piano.

When the lid is opened on a grand piano, for example, placing a stereo configuration with a considered SRA at around a metre or so away from the lid (so facing side on from the opened lid and piano) can capture an airy sound in the low part of the spectrum with a well-defined low end, without being overly resonant or overbearing. Using an equivalence stereo technique, such as DIN, EBS or ORTF, on the other hand, 30cm above the centre of the frame where the hammers and soundboard meet, can capture a full-bodied, resonant tone with definition and clarity. Getting closer to the hammers can help when you wish to emphasise the mechanical noise.

Many engineers like to place stereo configurations towards the back of the strings and the frame, but from the side where the lid opens, as again this can yield a very pleasing result in terms of resonance and tone, but with less chance of mechanical noise from the hammers being an issue. You can, of course, take the lid off a grand piano, and just as we discussed when working with an upright, you can experiment with where you place individual microphones and various stereo configurations. Like with many instruments, the purpose of experimenting and placing microphones is to listen and develop an understanding of how the instrument works, its mechanics and what sound is emanating from where.

Multi-microphone array based on one of the many configurations cited by Michael Williams and Guillaume Le Dû in their 2000 paper 'Multichannel Microphone Array Design (MMAD)'. The array was used to record Claude Debussy's prelude 'La cathédrale engloutie' with the specific intention of reproducing it in surround sound over five speakers. A combination of DPA 4011 condenser microphones with cardioid polar response patterns (front triplet coverage/array) and AKG C451 E microphones (back pair/rear of array) was used. Played back over five speakers the reproduced sound gave the impression that the music was enveloping the listener, like a big hug. The reverberation characteristic captured was a noticeable improvement over stereo recordings and sound localisation was also impressive. The distance between the microphones and piano allowed for the sound to propagate, capturing a more natural, rounded and balanced spectral tone.

DOUBLE BASS (UPRIGHT BASS)

I love recording the double bass and that is why I have singled it out for individual treatment. The information provided here will also help when you approach recording other instruments such as the cello.

As with many other instruments, although you may lose some detail, you only need to use one microphone to capture the instrument as a whole. Here, as is always the case with an acoustic instrument, it is all about finding an appropriate sounding space to record in, one with acoustic energy and where the characteristic of the room does not colour the recording unfavourably for the production aesthetic you are trying to achieve. Normally you want to find a spot where the sound of the instrument has had time to propagate through the room and you can attain a good balanced tone, so that when you listen to the recording via speakers or headphones the instrument sounds balanced across the frequency range.

Alternatively you can approach recording it with multiple microphones to capture and emphasise the mechanical noise and different resonant tones emanating from the various parts of the instrument, such as the neck and body. This in turn can be broken down even more in terms of the anatomy of the instrument and its specific parts, such as the bridge, F-holes and the body, comprising the upper and lower bout. These various areas can be used as a point of focus when it comes to choosing what microphone to use and how this should be placed in order to capture specific tones.

Such sounds can be mixed together and the recording or mix engineer can then balance the various sounds captured via the microphones to blend the different spectral content. This can be useful on many levels as it provides the engineer with options in terms of the detail they wish to push to the forefront of the mix. Simply by adjusting the various levels of the different microphones being used to capture a specific aspect of the sound, space can be made within the listening sound-stage for other instruments to sit. It can also be used to alter the perceived size and placement

Basic microphone placement when recording piano

Popular configurations and placements for recording a grand piano include XY90 or XY110 placed about 75–90cm above the centre of the hammers and tuning pins. Position a spaced pair, perhaps using cardioid polar response patterns instead of omni, with 60cm or a little more between the microphones, angled between the treble strings and bass strings. This should be just in front of where the soundboard and bridges join, so that when viewed from the sissde of the piano with the lid up, the microphone positioned over the bass strings will appear nearer to the rear of the piano than the microphone placed over the treble strings.

When using the Blumlein technique tilted at the side of the piano facing towards the centre of the strings, the configuration can be aligned so that one of the microphones faces directly towards the centre of the strings. (Imagine using MS and pointing the mid 'sum' microphone towards the strings, but in this instance use two figure of eight polar patterns instead of a cardioid and a figure of eight, though there is no harm in experimenting with MS.)

of the instrument within the listening soundstage or as part of a more considered vision for a mix. Creative dynamic processing can be used to bring parts of the overall spectral balance and tone out of the mix that may often get lost or naturally decay. You may, for example, wish to emphasise any slides, slaps or general mechanical noise generated by fingering on the neck and fingerboard.

If you only have one microphone to use, then a sensitive ribbon or condenser placed around 1m away from the instrument, facing just above the bridge, can yield a nice balanced tone. If you do not have a good sounding space to work with, however, and have access to a goose-neck style, small diaphragm condenser microphone with a specialist clip-on fitting, then placing the microphone under the bridge between the strings and body can provide a very usable result, as positioning it here will provide performance articulation, such as the 'bite' of the strings when plucked, and a decent amount of low end. Such small diaphragm microphones can also be placed closer to the F-hole.

If you choose to use any stereo techniques, it is best to choose a coincident, intensity/level difference stereo technique for phase coherence. MS works well as it is 100 per cent mono compatible. If you have an interesting room to work in then the side channels can be used to open up the listening soundstage during the recording or post-production.

An upright bass being recorded via a Brauner Phantom V large diaphragm condenser microphone set to an omnidirectional polar response pattern and placed 60cm away from the F-hole on the bass. Another large diaphragm condenser, an Avantone CK6, has been placed behind the bass at a distance of around 1.2m. There was no orthodox reasoning for this placement. After experimenting with positioning the microphone everyone agreed that it sounded good. There was a sweet spot where the sound of the bass within the live room resonated and added some additional ambience, which complemented the detail captured by the Brauner microphone when the polarity of the signal was inverted.

GENELEC

7

RE-AMPING AND RECORDING AS SOUND DESIGN

Re-amping can be used for both creative and corrective purposes. The process at its most basic usually, but not always, involves sending a pre-recorded signal through a re-amping box, which works by converting a line level, low impedance signal, which is balanced, into an unbalanced high impedance instrument signal level. The signal coming out of the re-amping box may then be fed into a guitar amp (bass, electric guitar, keyboard amp and so on) or a selection of amps, speakers and preamps, as well as a combination of guitar effects (FX) pedals, outboard or a combination of all of these.

When using a pre-record signal as described above, for example, the signal now arriving at a guitar amp via the re-amping box can be crafted after the performance by the musician, engineer or producer.

One or more microphones are then used to capture the sound emanating from the amp and record the tone crafted by the practitioner, which can be anything deemed suitable for the production at hand. This approach can take the pressure off what needs to be captured at the recording stage and can be a very creative process in more ways than one, something we will discuss in more detail in this chapter. For now, however, let's look at why re-amping may have to be a consideration during certain tracking sessions.

Many performers playing instruments such as an electric guitar, electric bass or a synth choose, or are directed by the engineer, to record and track via a DI box for a variety of reasons, including logistical concerns where spill can become an issue.

If a studio live room does not have isolation booths or separate live rooms for recording multiple instruments simultaneously, and the session brief requires recordings with zero or minimal spill, then using DI boxes can often provide a solution.

In this scenario the 'direct inject' method allows musicians to effectively plugin and play without having to use amplification and risk spill. Instead, when musicians wish to track together in the live room, or with some housed in the control room, DI boxes allow the recording engineer to take the high impedance, unbalanced instrument level signals and plumb them into a mixing console or preamp.

Appropriate gain staging can then be applied to the signal and fed back out to the performers as part of a foldback mix.

This allows musicians to play in the same room as a drummer, for example, so that body language, eye contact and the physical presence of the band playing live together can help achieve a feel that may be compromised if the musicians were otherwise forced to record and overdub sections of an arrangement bit by bit, or even via tracking and layering one instrument at a time.

At its most basic, re-amping is a functional process. In the example of a bass, synth or electric guitar captured solely by a DI box, although some have quality transformers or other components to help enhance the tone, the engineer can feed a pre-recorded signal back through an appropriate amp that can be tweaked until the desired sound is crafted. There is an argument that by re-amping the engineer can often push

A pre-recorded bass part captured solely via a DI box is being fed into an Ampeg bass amp via the Palmer Daccapo DI re-amping box. The re-amped sound is then being captured via a C414 microphone and recorded back into the DAW project.

the envelope and parameters of a given amp to its limits in the quest to shape a sound that stands out. For one you can turn the gain and level up to full, something that may otherwise be unpractical and deafen a performer if they had to be housed in the same room. You can, of course, achieve the latter by having a guitarist play in the control room and feed the signal directly into the amp housed in the live room, if you want to crank the sound up at the recording stage.

As well as the basic function of re-amping, whether through a guitar amp, a particular preamp or a piece of hardware known for adding additional tone and colour, an engineer can use the process of re-amping for sound design and, for example, drum replacement. The latter can be used in both a corrective and creative manner.

Plugins are available to help the user replace, repair or add extra samples and sounds to an existing recorded drum sound. There is, however, something quite satisfying and rewarding about using an amp and physical drum for this purpose.

In the example shown here, a snare drum has been placed on top of the amp. A pre-recorded and edited snare drum, perhaps gated to reduce spill, is then isolated from the rest of a recording or mix and fed to the amp via the re-amping box.

Each time the edited snare drum plays through the speaker at an appropriate level, the SPL it generates acts as a sudden pulse, and in turn this excites the snare drum and sounds like someone hitting the drum. Just like magic we have a ghost drummer in the room.

Well, not quite, but the resulting sound can be quite effective if the pulse or, more specifically, the beat, sounding as a burst of energy through the speaker to create the sudden change in air pressure, is not overly complex and regular. The sound of the snare drum being hit can then be recorded back into the project via a variety of microphones, if so desired. Adding such re-amped layers of your newly recorded snare, either as an add-on to your pre-recorded or programmed snare or as a supplement to bolster the overall tone, is only really touching the surface.

Re-amping a pre-recorded snare drum. The snare sound being played through the speaker is used to change the air pressure in the vicinity of the drum. The excitation of the drum via a burst of sound (specifically a sudden change in SPL) acts in a manner roughly similar to a drummer hitting the drum skin. The process can be used as a form of drum replacement, but can also be used creatively when different sounds are passed through the speaker and a resonant instrument. In this instance the recording is more akin to sound design.

There are really no rules when it comes to creative re-amping. You can use the process to play a pre-recorded sound through an interesting sounding space and use that environment's acoustics to add a unique reverberation characteristic to your productions. This could be achieved anywhere from a tiled bathroom to a cave. If you spend some time here varying the level in such an environment, which will ultimately vary the sound pressure levels generated from a given speaker, then the reverberation characteristic will be altered in the various spaces you choose to re-amp and

record in. From experience, experimentation can lead to many 'happy accidents'.

There are also the principles of acoustic and Helmholtz resonance to consider. Various musical instruments, paraphernalia, apparatus and materials can resonate sympathetically when a frequency that matches the object's natural frequency of resonance is passed through it at a considered sound pressure level.

You will have come across a Helmholtz resonator on many occasions, possibly without knowing it, for example when blowing into a bottle.

In reality such resonators are tuned, acoustic absorbers and are normally carefully designed to hone in on a particularly problematic frequency.

In a practical application, for example, they are used to minimise an issue with a standing wave, or more likely waves, at a variety of frequencies and room modes when the frequencies' wavelengths match the dimensions of a room and therefore build up and naturally amplify in a given space. Such problematic frequencies before acoustic treatment, for example by a Helmholtz resonator, can impact critical listening or unfavourably colour the characteristic of a live room, creating issues when recording.

However, means of working with the principle of acoustic resonance, using EQ to sweep through the frequency spectrum and/or using a variety of amps with different frequency responses, can all be considered potential ways to help us find and manipulate the natural resonant frequency or set of frequencies of a given instrument or enclosure, which can in turn be used to generate some interesting tones and overtones.

Again, I strongly recommend that you read more on the subject to unravel my concise and possibly simplistic summations.

From a practical point of view it is once again about experimentation. Take the photo where a snare drum has been placed lying on its side on top of the bass amp. Initially the snare was put on the amp and an edited and isolated snare sound was then passed through the amp to excite the snare drum and create the phantom ghost drummer. However, why not try feeding a vocal through the amp and drum and see how that sounds, depending on which side the drum is facing (batter head or snare head) and whether the snare is engaged or not. It can lead to some interesting rattles, fuzz and distortion. Or how about feeding a synth bass through the amp and a metal bin? If you play with the settings on the amp and swap the snare for other resonant instruments, such as different size drums or an acoustic guitar, and then isolate and send the various sounds and instruments from the project through the set up, you can turn recording into sound design. This is arguably just one facet when we discuss the art of recording as practitioners.

I have used re-amping on many occasions. Placing speakers against the soundboard of a piano, for example, and feeding a vocal through

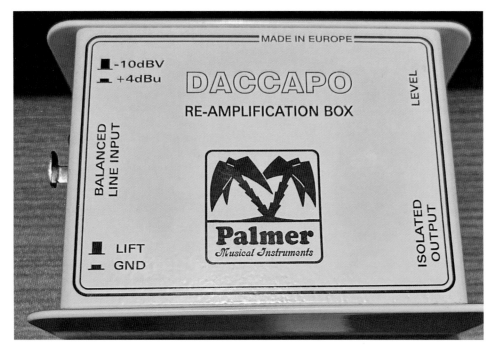

Palmer Daccapo re-amping box.

Re-amping is more than just using a guitar amp at the end of the outgoing signal chain to craft a tone. The ¼in Otari reel to reel tape machine seen here was picked up for free from an old client and has been used for re-amping on many occasions. Along with the tonal character you may expect from driving levels going to tape at certain frequencies, there is a built-in speaker that I used to love playing through and then capturing its sound via a closely placed microphone alongside the direct output of the tape machine.

the piano at high sound pressure levels generated some interesting resonant tones. I have also had fun sending sampled strings via different aux buses or a designated foldback system into different size speakers. The speakers can then be arranged to place the various sounds within a space that ideally has a noticeable RT60 time and reverberation characteristic. Recording the sounds with natural reverberation back in to your project and automating between the dry and wet string sounds can help introduce movement, space and depth to the mix.

8

WORKING WITH MULTIPLE MICROPHONES, EDITING AND PREPARING FOR A MIX

When mixing is viewed, perhaps in its most simplest form, as the process of placing, balancing and blending sounds together, then arguably that makes many recording engineers, by its very nature, mixing engineers.

We have discussed how multiple microphones are often utilised in order to capture parts of a given instrument and, when combined, an overall tone or spectral balance of a given sound and instrument. This is in its very essence mixing, as recording engineers train their ears and learn with practice how to choose and place appropriate microphones in order to blend together the sounds emanating from a sound source. Sometimes very little is needed after the sounds have been balanced and placed within the listening soundstage.

Arguably, though, these are practical considerations and not all recording techniques are viewed in a similar manner to the creative decisions, such as when a mix engineer becomes something like a storyteller and uses a variety of resources to craft a production that the end user, the listener, will enjoy. Nevertheless, the way in which a recording engineer works can hugely impact the final quality of the production.

Unless otherwise specified by the project manager – the producer in many instances – it is good practice for a recording engineer to pass the multitracks to the mix engineer edited and ready to mix.

We can compare the stages of a record being made to that of sculpting. Initially a recording engineer will capture as much as possible with the most suitable materials at their disposal, as if it were a big block of wood or ice.

The recording engineer then starts to chip away at the block and clean it up before the mix engineer takes over and plays with the shape. The record at this point can be seen as beginning to tell the story. Sounds within the listening soundstage have a size, energy and placement. They are not static and dynamics are noticeable not just in terms of how loudly or quietly an instrument, sound or passage of music is played, but in terms of space and movement, which some may suggest could be considered as spatial dynamics.

Once the mix engineer has helped the block of ice take its shape and form, through balancing and blending various elements for cohesion and achieving an artistic aesthetic, a mastering engineer can step in to add the final gloss and make sure that the final work is presentable in terms of format requirements and standards. As in the case of ice or wood sculpture, it is now ready to be put on show for everyone to see.

In order to get the material ready to sculpt, or in our case mix, though, a recording engineer must first consider a few tasks and processes that can be viewed as falling into the categories of creative or corrective practice. Some of these processes you would be expected to consider and apply as part of your specific role as a recording engineer, while others you may well need to carry out under the direction of the producer.

There are many approaches to how we facilitate a recording session. For many reasons it is fairly common practice for practitioners to record multiple takes and then edit together and compile, or 'comp' for short, the best of those takes to create one overall take with which the producer and artist are happy. Choosing the best takes can be based on many factors, such as tuning, performance articulation, timing, energy and feel.

Some mix engineers and producers will request all the various multitracks and takes so that they can oversee the edits themselves. Even when a recording engineer is expected to complete such edits, additional alternative takes may still need to be accessible at a later stage in the mix process, when creative editing may be applied by the producer and/or mix engineer. In essence, the process of 'comping' can be viewed as both creative and corrective practice. Corrective practice can, for example, involve finding takes to replace a section where a performance or technical error has taken place, perhaps a mishit of a drum or a microphone cutting out due to a faulty cable. A creative application of the process, using the example of a drum recording, may be to piece together and comp multiple drum fills to create a part that was never played by the drummer, at least not as first intended and as a part of the initial performance.

When it comes to comping, continuity is one of many considerations. Does the comp make sense musically and technically? The former usually pertains to performance feel and articulation, whereas the latter can be as simple as making sure that the transitions between the various parts you have compiled sound natural with no clicks or pops, and where nothing suddenly cuts out, like the ringing out of a cymbal, or when there are huge discrepancies in dynamics and levels between the chosen takes.

There are also considerations when it comes to tuning. Again this is why it is often good practice to ask performers to check the tuning of their instruments between takes, which is something many professional drummers consider, as well as other musicians playing pitched instruments.

It is also generally the job of the recording engineer to 'top' and 'tail' the recordings by editing out any unwanted noise, such as talking between takes or electrical noise. You would also be

Overtone Labs tune-bot drum tuner. It is often about attention to detail and taking time to get the sound right at the source.

expected to apply fades to help with smooth transitions between takes and at the start and end of various musical passages.

Perhaps one of the most understated considerations when prepping a multitrack recording for mixing, or so I have found when working with some of my students, is the concept of phase coherence.

This is possibly because many of them did not think it was a concern and have often worked mainly 'in the box' with samples, midi and software-based instruments rather than multiple microphones set up to capture a given sound source.

It is worth noting that all the issues pertaining to phase coherence, namely the destructive interference that can audibly manifest in a manner that distorts the stereophonic image and tone of a sound, mostly but not exclusively occurs when an engineer sets up multiple microphones. If the issues are not addressed in a project then it can have an impact on the effectiveness of how various tools, techniques and processes enhance the listening soundstage during the mix process.

What is destructive interference and how does it impact recording? Put simply, phase coherence (see 'phase' and 'phase shift' in the Glossary) is the relationship between two or more waveforms and destructive interference occurs when there is an issue with the relationship between them, and more specifically what occurs when these wave-forms are added or 'summed' together.

From a practical point of view, recording engi-neers tend to consider phase coherence when using multiple microphones to capture a given instrument. More specifically we are concerned with time differ-ences and phase shifts, the point when a sound and its related waveform complete a whole cycle of peak and trough, or 'high pressure' and 'low pressure', as the waves arrive at the microphone diaphragm.

Phase coherence and destructive interference can manifest, for example, when recording a drum kit, a guitar amp or in any situation when more than one microphone has been used on a specific sound source, instrument or soundstage.

Many recording engineers take such concepts and phenomena into consideration when setting up micro-phones and will invert the polarity of incoming signals to minimise issues such as frequency cancelation. In Chapter 5 it was suggested that a good starting point here is to flip the polarity (normally 180 degrees) of any microphone facing in an opposing direction to the other microphones being used. If, for example, the microphones are placed close to the rim of the top of the snare drum, facing towards the drum, then invert the polarity of the microphone below the snare facing upwards. If you choose to place a microphone at the back of a guitar amplifier with an open back, again make sure you flip the polarity if you have micro-phones placed facing the front of the speaker.

Again, just to recap, if one microphone diaphragm is facing in the opposite direction to the other, then the peaks and troughs of the incoming waveform repre-sented as a change in voltage, after being converted from a change in air pressure by the transducer of the microphone, are moving in opposing direc-tions. Ideally we want waveforms to complement one another and to move in the same direction, if you like. In this way when they are summed together they will sound louder, reinforced and fuller in tone, as opposed to causing some frequencies to be cancelled, or perhaps more accurately attenuated. The latter causes the tone to be thinner and lacking any weight or body, most noticeably in the lower frequency ranges. Total frequency cancellation only occurs when two identical opposing waveforms are summed together. Here mid-side (intensity stereo) coincident level difference stereo would be a good example as the sides or 'difference' are identical with one channel having the polarity inverted. This again is why stereo recording techniques such as MS (sum and difference level difference/intensity stereo) are ideal in any recording situation because there is no concern about folding a mix down from stereo to mono.

Two basic sine waves of the same frequency with one inverted would also cause 100 per cent cancellation if summed together. In reality, however, the waveforms you are dealing with when record-ing various instruments are complex on many levels. Application of the mathematical process called Fourier analysis reveals that all audio wave-forms are complex patterns made up of a number of simpler waveforms, specifically sine waves summed together. When, however, amplitude differentials and the envelope or shape of the sound being recorded are taken into account, as well as the impact that room acoustics have on a record-ing, then it becomes clear that the idea of perfect phase coherence is impossible, at least in the pre-digital domain. There are ways to map out a wave-form in the digital domain and then match it with other waveforms, but arguably this is doctoring the sounds you have painstakingly set about recording.

This is worth considering as the process of edit-ing audio via time-alignment to enhance phase cohesion is far from foolproof. We need to be aware that it is about minimising issues pertaining to phase coherence and destructive interference, and we will never correct 100 per cent of these issues. It is about learning to use our ears and decide what sounds best, since playing with processes such as time alignment does not always enhance the recorded audio and can in reality make things worse.

Before even considering time alignment or 'phase alignment' as a method, it is best to understand right from the start, when recording with multiple microphones, that more needs to be taken into consideration than just frequency cancellation when it comes to the listening soundstage and the virtual images created over two or more speakers. No two microphones are identically the same in terms of frequency and transient response. Using a diaphragm of some sort is in essence a mechanical function and so there will be variations in how well sound pressure levels are converted to voltage via the transducer.

Many engineers choose to use different models and types of microphones in order to capture different tones of a given instrument and the room itself. Even without considering time of arrival differences at the various microphones placed around a given instrument or space, there will always be variations in how the waveforms are being captured. The differences in the readings of transients and their associated frequencies, for example, would sum together in a manner that immediately compromises any concept of true coherence, at least in terms of parity.

When viewed through this lens, correcting issues with phase, other than the really obvious audible distortions, becomes a point of taste. Training your ears to listen out for issues that may manifest due to destructive interference is a skill that you will develop with time and practice.

Before looking at the process of time or phase alignment, and describing how and why you can use such a technique, or process if you prefer, in order to edit and enhance the recorded audio, I would like to focus on an element of destructive interference that does not get as much attention as it should, at least in my opinion.

This is the concept of image distortion. There are many excellent publications on this subject and I highly recommend reading anything by Michael Williams, who cites the idea of 'Angular Distortion' when discussing SRAs. In the simplest of explanations, angular distortion can be pictured as the recorded sound source being either squeezed or overly hyped and exaggerated between two or more speakers. Though this can be viewed as distortion relating to how two or more microphones are carefully configured and placed in a specific and thought-out manner in order to capture a sound source with considered localisation cues. Image distortion can also be a phenomenon when dealing with multiple microphones that are placed in an uncorrelated manner.

When recording a drum kit, for example, you may have chosen to use three microphones to capture the kick drum and three to capture the snare. You may have then also chosen to place microphones on the hi-hats and toms, and then use a stereo configuration as overheads to capture an image of the whole drum kit and cymbals. Alongside this you may well have also set up some microphones to capture the ambience of the room. Now I don't think there is such a thing as a microphone whisperer, but you certainly cannot tell the room microphones or overheads not to pick up the kick drum, or indeed tell the kick drum microphones to pick up only that drum. There are, of course, tools such as noise gates, expanders and transient designers that can be used fairly effectively in some situations and circumstances, depending on where the microphones are placed, but the 'chattering' caused by the opening and closing of a dynamic processor such as a noise gate is not conducive to capturing a natural-sounding, well-tuned, resonant and balanced drum recording when the full drum kit is viewed as one whole instrument.

The point here is that you will get spill from one drum into the microphone intended for another drum, or via the overheads or room microphones. Unless you apply some sort of time adjustment or delay alongside the polarity inversion, then there will be time of arrival discrepancies as well as potential issues with phase shifts being different at the microphone diaphragms. In some circumstances if these time of arrival differences are not taken into consideration then it is possible that the overall image of the sound will be blurred when the various waveforms captured by the different microphones are summed together. It is not just a case of subtle frequency cancellation that can make recordings sound thinner, or more severe audible artefacts manifesting because of comb filtering occurring, but over speakers there is less chance of creating a solid and centred phantom image, or over headphones the mix of sounds can sound less like they are in the centre of your head, although arguably that is not always a bad thing.

Once you hear and identify image distortion in this manner it cannot be unheard, and with practice this is something you will train your ears to recognise.

Time alignment or phase alignment tools, as they are often referred to, are often used to rectify this very issue, but they can sometimes make an overall tone or image worse. Whether aligning waveforms manually or with a plugin within your chosen DAW, a good starting point is to pick a reference point on which to align all the other waveforms.

In the case of drums this will often be either the kick drum or the snare. If you chose the kick as your point of reference and have multiple microphones on the bass drum, it may be easier to choose the recording with the most distinct transients to align to, which in this example would be expected to be the microphone placed inside the bass drum, as in theory there should be less spill. In terms of what sounds best, however, and whether any alignment is actually required in the first place, well that's your call and it's all about practice and gaining experience.

You do not need to align every drum. It is often just about listening while slowly aligning parts of the kit one at a time until the overall sound in terms of tone and image is enhanced.

It is also good to be able to AB test the results before and after alignment. Sometimes the differences are very subtle or they might sound less effective in terms of what was already captured at source. On other occasions, however, the positive difference can be very noticeable in terms of the impact on the overall sound.

Another starting point for many engineers when recording a drum kit with multiple microphones may be to select the snare drum as the reference point and begin by listening to how the sound may be enhanced by aligning the overheads, for example. They will take phase coherence into consideration when setting up microphones and invert polarity at the source on one or more channels, but image distortion can be slightly more subtle in terms of working to create a more cohesive and centred phantom image.

A good starting point when considering phase coherence post-recording is to have all of your faders set flat to 0dB in accordance with the levels you have recorded at. In other words, do not take your faders up or down to boost or attenuate the level passing through the channel.

When demonstrating the phenomena to my students I have often used EQ on a channel to exaggerate the issues associated with destructive interference and demonstrate that EQ is not as effective as it should be in terms of tone shaping. I would suggest it is good practice to compare the relationships of the multiple waveforms captured by the various microphones in a form that is as pure as possible, precisely as it was recorded at source both in terms of level and panning.

This is simply to ensure that any decision you make in terms of how time/phase alignment enhances the recording is based on the recording at source and not on any enhancements achieved via spectral or dynamic processing. It is also good to have faders at the same level, Without any additional processing this is often when we can notice issues with sounds being summed together, such as a bass drum lacking in body and resonance. If you have one channel with additional spectral processing, either via EQ or a resonance tool, this can mask the issue to the untrained ear.

Another telltale sign that there are issues with phase coherence is when you move faders to similar values (recorded levels) and get an audible drop in level. You will notice that if you change the level of one or more faders this relationship will change. This is because there are fewer issues with cancellation or, more specifically, less destructive interference through summing said waveforms. This again is why you should start with the faders flat.

Correlation meters, sometimes with spectral analysis, can help you visually gauge that you have an issue with phase coherence. When looking at a meter, however, it can be unhealthy to become fixated on what you are seeing rather than what you are hearing. Generally if your mix sounds good and does not all but disappear when summed or 'folded' down to mono, then you have some room to manoeuvre.

Arguably a good reading on a dynamic stereo recording is anywhere between 0 (90 degrees) in the middle and +1 (0 degrees) to the right on a traditional pointer (needle gauge) correlation meter, or as a vertical meter with +1 of the type fitted to a Neve A246 recording console.

If your reading floats between +0.5 (45 degrees) and +1 this is often considered as healthy. Whether at the recording stage or during post, you should hope that the listening soundstage is not static and has movement both in terms of level and spatial dynamics over the stereophonic image and the picture of sound being created for the listener.

If you are only getting a reading of +1 with no movement, then it is likely you are either taking a reading from a summed mono bus, that nothing in your mix is stereo or panned, or that you are only

Part of the meter bridge within the master section of a Neve A258 recording console. The 'pointer' style needle gauge correlation meter in the middle is sandwiched between two VU meters for the left and right master output.

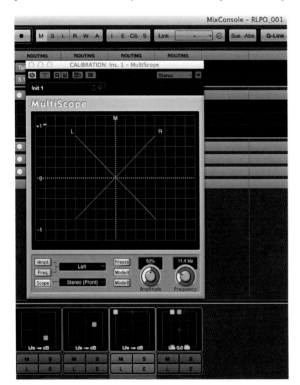

MultiScope meter in Nuendo. The correlation meter is situated to the left and gives a reading over a vertical meter.

looking at a single channel as opposed to comparing phase coherence between varied waveforms. If you attain a reading of –1 and it is not fluctuating, then the two signals you are comparing are identical and 180 degrees out of polarity from one another. A situation like this occurs when measuring the side channel (difference) of an MS configuration, for instance, but otherwise it is very unlikely you would come across such a scenario. Some studio hardware measuring phase coherence and speaker systems can be accidentally wired out of polarity on occasion, but that is another consideration.

For the most part, if your correlation meter is providing readings that fluctuate anywhere between 0 and –1 (180 degrees) then you need to redress some of your decisions about phase coherence and the sum of the chosen sounds. Certain plugins and tools deliberately play with phase coherence, namely delay and polarity, or more specifically phase shifts, in order to create a sense of artificial width, so you need to be mindful of the impact on your mix when using such tools. There are also psychoacoustic considerations such as the Haas effect or 'precedence effect', which have become increasingly popular with mix engineers trying to open up a mix and create artificial stereo via manipulating localisation cues. Dr Helmut Haas discovered that certain delayed sounds interact in a manner that is not perceived as an echo if they arrive at the ear within 20 to 40ms of the most direct sound wave arriving at the ears. Such differences are helpful for localising sound based on level differences or intensity, but at such short time differences from the initial direct sound arriving at the ear that they fall below what has been coined the 'echo threshold'. Applying such concepts with little understanding can again cause issues when it comes to phase coherence.

Before handing files to another practitioner to mix or carry out any other process, a recording engineer should really consider time/phase alignment. Some of the concerns cited can arise anytime you are working with multiple channels to capture the same source. For example, if you use a DI box on a bass and then employ the 'thru' to parallel the sound to a bass amp and record via a microphone at the same time, or whether you look towards re-amping a bass part already recorded via a DI at a later date, then you need to look at the relationship between the different waveforms captured.

In the screenshots here time alignment has been applied manually using tools within the chosen DAW, in this case Pro Tools. There are some excellent plugins that help with this process and arguably they are far more accurate, but the manual approach can be a very visual way in which to understand the relationship between the various waveforms. In this instance five different microphone are being used to capture the sound of a guitar amp within a large live room. The first two microphones were dynamic microphones positioned no more than 2cm away from the speakers in the amp (a Shure SM57 facing on axis to one of the two speakers and a Sennheiser MD 441 on axis to the other speaker).

The third microphone was a large diaphragm condenser with a cardioid setting placed about 1m away from the amp, slightly raised up and tilted to face, on axis, the reflective wooden floor. The fourth and fifth microphones were two pencil condenser microphones placed coincident to one another at 90 degrees to form a level difference stereo (intensity stereo) configuration.

Before the various waveforms were phase aligned, or more specifically moved and time aligned, the overall summed sound was one that sounded blurred over the stereo image and lacked any noticeable low end tone. By contrast the aligned audio provided a solid centre image and the tone had a deeper, more defined low end and sonorous tone with body and weight.

It also helped in this circumstance to utilise a level difference stereo configuration with coincident placement of the pencil considers, since overall this source point placement without any time arrival differences is easier to align with the various individual/mono channel microphones used to capture different tonal aspects of the amp.

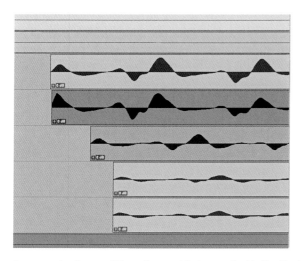 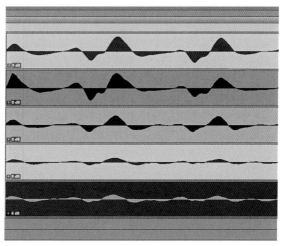

An example of manual time alignment being applied in Pro Tools. Five different microphones are being used to capture the sound of a guitar amp. The time of arrival differences are evident when you cut out the audio at the point when you can find a distinctive transient to use as a reference point.

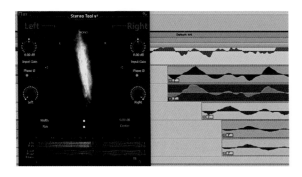
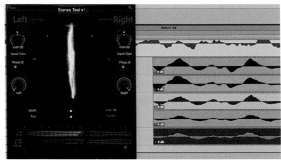

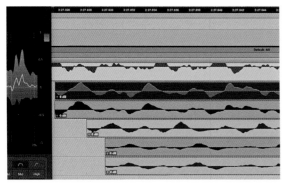
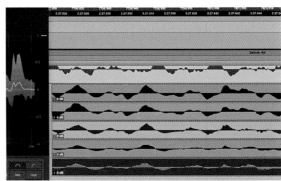

Two types of correlation meter displaying different information. In the screenshots it is evident that after time alignment that the readings provided by the correlation meters, Stereo tool by Flux and the Metric AB by ADPTR Audio Systems with a reading of phase coherence over the frequency spectrum, have moved to a reading ever so closer to +1.

The readings highlighted in the different types of correlation meters pictured here would suggest that only slight differences were occurring in terms of phase coherence before and after manual phase/time alignment. This is why it is important to use your ears as I found that the differences were anything but subtle.

It is also worth noting that on this occasion there was no need to adjust the polarity of the waveforms.

As the name should suggest, when you are looking at the process of phase/time alignment you should be considering both the time differences and the phase angle of the waveforms being summed together. They are not exclusive and both work together to impact the overall tone and image of a given sound being created virtually over two speakers or headphones.

Once again, though, it is worth noting that such alignment can make a sound source less pleasing for many reasons after being applied, either by a plugin or manually. You really have to use your ears and be decisive.

Students have often asked me how the sense of space and depth captured by a microphone is impacted when we play with phase and time alignment. The confusion here is generally centred around the idea that, by moving a recorded waveform captured via a microphone that was initially positioned and intended as an ambient microphone a distance away from the chosen reference point, we are altering the actual recorded sound. This is not the case.

Localisation cues can be impacted when playing with alignment (for example, in the context of summing mono microphones with stereo configurations), especially if we do not pan the microphones in relation to the same perspective as that in which the stereo microphone configuration or array is facing in terms of the record soundstage. You are not altering the ratio between the direct and reverberant sound being captured by the ambient microphone, or more specially the recorded waveform you are actually moving. So you are not changing the sound of the recording in that way. The microphone channel and the recording effectively still sounds like a room microphone that is a distance away from the sound source you are recording.

QUANTISATION AND TUNING

This is an area that I do not want to cover in too much detail. Firstly because it does not always fall under the remit of the recording engineer within modern production methods, and secondly because I feel passionately that a big part of the art of recording is working towards capturing something that stands out at the source, not only in terms of the sonic quality of the recording itself, but also in the context of documenting a great and possibly unique performance in terms of articulation, expression and dynamics. The point is that there is something very honest about recording, something human and organic, for want of a better word.

Some of my favourite records are not perfectly in time or tune in line with some modern production values, but they sound great and they make me feel good listening to them.

I would also suggest that most modern producers working in the box are aware of what quantisation is. Just to be clear, however, it is very different to the time or phase alignment discussed previously in this chapter. One pertains to how a musical performance feels and sounds in relation to timing, specifically either in relation to a set grid (based on a time signature(s) and tempo) as a reference or in relation to another instrument to lock within the arrangement. The other concerns the quality of the summed audio in terms of tone and image.

Possibly it is too simplistic to suggest that one is associated with the art of sound and the other with its science, although arguably both principles could cross disciplines.

If you have to quantise maybe just work on very short specific sections, if you can, or if you are working with rigid elements in a backing track

Alignment tips when tracking

If you know you will be working with multiple microphones at various distances from one another to capture a given sound source, and do not have access to plugins to help with alignment, then ask the musician(s) to play a single audible sound that can be used to align the waveforms. Here a clap or hit of a drum is ideal. Record something with a distinct transient to use as a reference point when you need to align waveforms manually.

Be aware when viewing a computer screen that often the graphic user interface (GUI) is not a true representation of the recorded sound. Judgements about inverting/flipping the polarity of a waveform should be based on how it sounds collectively, when the summing of the various waveforms is being listened to, rather than what you see on the screen.

that have been programmed to a grid, you could possibly look at extracting a groove from the newly recorded audio and use that as a reference to tighten up other elements of your arrangement.

Try to avoid using 100 per cent values when applying quantisation or, for that matter, tuning.

When it comes to recording drums, it is often worth taking note of fundamental frequencies if the drummer is using devices such as a tune-bot. This is useful in case you wish to use drum replacement in a creative manner, inserting additional samples to layer with your recorded drums and enhance resonance and overtones, as you can then look at tuning the samples to blend in with your recording.

By asking your drummer to play individual hits before or after a session you can also use these hits for any restorative or corrective work such as sound replacement when you need to repair a mishit or faulty channel previously noticed during recording.

Finally, after any tuning or quantisation it may be worth using a plugin to double check the time and phase alignment in case any editing has impacted your previous work.

9
FOOD FOR THOUGHT

Rich Thair
(Red Snapper, The Aloof, Number, Petwo Evans, Dicky Continental)

I have spent 30 years in recording studios in the UK and Europe, with my various bands, writing, mixing, editing and recording. I have been lucky enough to have worked with some amazing engineers and programmers over the years and as a producer I feel that I have developed the skills and confidence to have established myself with my own sound and approach.

From a band/live studio perspective, I think the key is to be well rehearsed and have a clear idea of how you want things to sound, both at source but also at the final mix stages. That said, my whole approach over the years has been to be as open minded and experimental as possible.

I do feel that sometimes the original idea is often the best and if that means the sound of instruments at the demo stage, then don't be frightened to go with that sound/recording.

As a producer and musician I am constantly listening to music, old and current. I listen a lot to my back catalogue and always use this research as an important learning tool when working on new material.

I listen to my own and other people's music on as many speakers/headphones as possible, in as many environments as possible.

There are traditional rules and guidelines in the world of studio recording but, as in life, sometimes rules are there to be broken, adapted and twisted.

The whole process of producing music should be fun, exciting, emotional, passionate and creative. Be patient and never forget why you chose to make music.

Darren Jones (engineer and producer)
(including for Stormzy, Frank Turner and Emeli Sandé)

Trust your instincts, allow yourself to be confident. Second guesses often turn out to be wrong.

Simon Gogerly (engineer and producer)
(including for Paloma Faith, Underworld and U2)

Make a collection of unusual equipment: small speakers, tape machines, odd pedals, children's instruments and so on. Then use them to sample, re-amp and mangle audio. Anything that can give your sound a unique edge is good. Don't always take the easy option; experiment and have fun playing with sound.

Paul Winter-Hart
(Kula Shaker)

When recording with Rick Rubin at Ocean Way in Hollywood he brought in a big, smooth stone and placed it on top of the padding in the kick drum. He said it helped focus the sound. A brick will do this too, though a denser stone is better.

I also like to use a business card or similar, taped to the batter head where the beater hits. Also, depending on the genre, tuning the snare low can really sound good with damping.

You have to have some faith in the engineer/producer to get everything to sound good. That's a combination of gear, playing, the room, and the vibe.

The last one is important. I think experienced people know how to not get in the way of that, that is to facilitate the flow of the creative process.

I think the Glyn Johns technique is obviously good for simplicity and those with limited mic choices. I remember getting good results with Steve Harris in a very high tech place called the Pierce Room behind the Hammersmith Odeon. He used two Coles microphones [4038s] as 'underheads', at a height just above the knee, and about an arm's span away placed either side of the kit, outside the cymbals, but not too high to catch too much of them.

Brendan Lynch
(Ocean Colour Scene, Paul Weller, Primal Scream)

Sometimes the demo is better than the version you recorded in the fancy studio. The performance, feel and sound of that thing was impossible to recreate.

Richard Marcangelo (session drummer)
(including Robert Plant, Manfred Mann's Earth Band and Chris Rea)

My first 'big' recording session was in 1978 at Scorpio Studios for the Bowles Bros (band) on the Decca label produced by the legendary West Coast producer Bones Howe.

The engineer was Dennis Weinreich, another American. We spent at least three months on and off in the studio as a young band laying backing tracks … all playing together.

I learnt so much about tuning and dampening of the drum kit from Dennis as I soon realised he knew how to get a great drum sound in the room.

As house engineer in one of London's top studios he obviously had all the best drummers coming through the studio and had learnt how to tune and dampen a drum kit to get the required sound for the style of music being recorded. We didn't play to a click/metronome, so I had a massive introduction into how 'time/tempo' was so important in getting a great track together. Bones was a great source of information and advice for all of us young musicians and performers starting our careers.

Tuning and dampening are so crucial to getting not only a good drum sound but a drum sound which is applicable to the style of music being recorded.

Tuning and dampening varies a lot from style to style. Drum tuning is often called a bit of a 'dark art' because there are so many variables attached to the process. The sound of a drum changes so much depending on the room you are in. Small spaces are not the best for a good sound, though in my experience there are certain booths in studios that do have a good dry sound with fewer ugly overtones. Ugly overtones, especially from the snare, are usually present when there is a low ceiling and square or rectangular walls where 'standing waves' are present.

As a rule of thumb, high tuning is preferred by jazz drummers, speed metal and thrash, Drum 'n' bass artists or any music that uses fast tempos where you need short sounds that don't 'bleed' into each other. High tuning makes it easier to play 'double strokes' where you need that 'bounce' off the drum head. Mid and low range tuning is applicable to lots other styles like rock/pop/funk/reggae/hip hop/soul/r'n'b/country and so on.

Another simple rule of thumb is that tuning the bottom head of a drum tighter than the top head will get you on the road to a decent sound. With a snare drum, the bottom head (snare head) can be a lot tighter, four or five times tighter than the top head (batter head). Toms are usually tuned to be certain intervals apart, depending on how many are being used. A 4th is a popular interval for tom toms.

Regarding dampening, I still think 'Moon Gel' is a great resource. It is incremental in that it's easy to put more on and then take off if it's too much. O rings are either on or off, so you don't have that leeway. With regard to cymbals, well, you can't tune a cymbal so it is what it is! Cheap cymbals are not nice! They sound cheap and I'd say it's better not to play them unless you are looking for a 'cheap' sound. Take them off the kit!

After getting as good a sound as possible through tuning and dampening (if required), then I think the headphone mix/balance is of most importance as it determines how comfortable you feel when playing. After a couple of years of getting more and more studio work I began to realise that there were some engineers who automatically seemed to get a lovely sound in the cans, almost like you were playing to a finished track with good levels and a pleasing stereo image and maybe some nice reverb on parts of the kit like toms and snare.

Then there were other engineers who just put the faders up and expected you to just accept what you heard. These sessions would be a bit of a struggle as you were continually asking for this up, that down and so on. Generally, I don't want any of the kit in my cans apart from a little kick drum maybe.

Kevan Gallagher (engineer and producer)
(Annie Lennox, Ronan Keating)

Pay no attention to how microphone positions 'look'. Pay every attention to how they sound.

Simon Mitchell
(Eone)

Sitting in a studio can be a magical experience, but so can the journey on the train to the studio. With the accessibility of technology, laptops or phones can now serve as portable studios. And if you hear some interesting sonics, try recording it with your device's built-in microphone. Add a ton of effects, and you've just made a unique atmospheric sound.

Linton Bennett (aka Stepz)
(Dido, Warren G, All Saints, Jamelia, Imogen Heap)

The studio is a creative environment at whatever stage of the recording process. It should allow you to critically discuss/adjust your song and actively listen to work without stimuli. If it doesn't work here then it's pretty much going to collect criticism.

Danny de Matos (Lisbon Kid)

My role as a producer is to make the biggest positive impact on the music possible. To make the output exceed the input. The sum being greater than the parts. It's to grow what is there, by adding to the narrative, so that the audience better understands the story. Sometimes it can be through bringing other influences, knowledge or techniques to the table. And this might be by contributing further creative ideas, be they compositional, technical, or in terms of the aesthetic. It's about doing what is required, but only that. So often this means a need to clarify, and to make concise. I always rehearse with an artist or band prior to going into the studio. We review all the existing parts and may well edit and reduce what is there, be that arrangement or structure, lyric or melody or harmony. I always say that for me, it's about getting it on the radio, and making something that will be remembered. We're trying to shift the world on its axis, if only by a tiny amount. Producing should be about making magic and making a difference. I'm always trying to make the 'magic difference'.

Lex Cameron (musician, producer and singer)

As a young singer working with legendary producer Reggie Lucas [Madonna and Miles Davis] I watched him build a snare sound from a sample of a pot being hit and some white noise. This changed my perception of sonics and it really sunk in that it's all just frequencies for us to manipulate in exciting ways.

Collaborate with different people on different styles of music, especially if it's a genre you're not used to as they'll have different mixing requirements and ways of achieving results, which will ultimately give you invaluable new knowledge, which will in turn only add to your musical evolution.

FINAL THOUGHTS

I wanted to finish this book where I started and reiterate that this work is intended for hobbyists and for practitioners starting out. Yes, there are some fancy looking studios and equipment pictured throughout, but it is the concept that counts and this book is a basic overview in many ways as I have chosen to focus on some of the basic building blocks and fundamentals to get you up and running.

There are many other theoretical concepts and technical details to consider and I recommend reading the articles, papers, journals and books written by and contributed to by many of the professional industry practitioners and academics I have cited – not to mention the many other authors who cover the vast range of related subjects I have omitted.

Above all else, I believe that recording is an art. Whether you are capturing a performance, a mood or a vibe, a moment in time or the recording itself as part of the sound design that influences the production's direction and aesthetic as a whole, recording is not a static process, nor should it be stifling. There are moments when technical detail and considerations can be paramount for specific applications and formats, but for the most part I encourage you to be creative and have fun with the process.

Interesting room acoustics, a collection of weird and wonderful instruments and the process of

creative re-amping alone can yield some noteworthy results that open up and colour the listening soundstage.

Don't just get used to setting up and placing your instruments in the same space within the rooms you regularly work in. In the first two photos in this section the drums have been set up in different areas of the live room: two different drummers with two different models of drum kits. It is at the beginning of a session that we get to choose the microphones, partly based on where a given instrument is placed within the room and what its impact is on the room sound itself.

Focusing on the kick, snare and hats. In this instance most of the desired sound came from moving the kit into a different place within the room

Often drummers will bring multiple snares to a session in order to pick an appropriate weight and sound for the genre and brief at hand. Many drummers will also spend time tuning to the room and may decide to dampen the drums. Engineers may also place baffle boards around the kit to alter the amount of reflections, room resonance and acoustic colouration. It may be that a certain style or design of kit from a particular era is required to really capture the essence of the production aesthetic at source. I have picked up some great vintage kits second hand for a bargain. They often need some tender loving care, but getting to refurbish and restore any instrument is a great way to get to know the instrument and such information can in turn unlock the best approaches to recording.

An sEElectronics Reflexion Filter being set up and used in an experimental manner alongside a Brauner Phantom V placed at the side of the kit. The idea was to see how well the filter could reduce some of the high frequency spill from the hi-hats when using a cardioid polar response pattern facing in line, on axis with the snare.

It really is often about keeping things simple. Less can be more. Use your ears. If it sounds and feels right there is no need to start overcomplicating a recording and possibly overprocessing the incoming signal. There is plenty of time in the mix to mess things up.

On many occasions it really is all about experimentation. As practitioners we can get used to our 'go to' choices for facilitating many aspects of the recording process, especially if we have a sound already in mind, and such a sound has been achieved successfully on previous occasions. To grow and develop, however, even the most seasoned professional is often looking to shake things up, and experimentation can be key.

I would also respectfully suggest that many recordings can be impacted, not always in a positive way, by overprocessing a signal at source. Just because you have access to various pieces of outboard to process a sound spectrally, spatially and dynamically, does not mean you have to use it. This is certainly why in part I have chosen to avoid discussing such signal chains and processing in any great detail, if at all.

When it comes to recording, less really can be more and keeping things simple is a good place to start. Using your ears to balance the sound within the listening soundstage just via the microphones at the source is a real art and a very pleasing experience, especially if you get the chance to work in controlled or interesting-sounding live rooms.

GLOSSARY

3:1 Rule If you know your work has to be mono compatible and find yourself setting up multiple microphones around different sound sources such as a choir, then it can be worth monitoring in mono (summed) to listen out for any issues with destructive interference, such as comb filtering.

As a very basic rule of thumb, the idea is that when recording with multiple microphones, you will achieve better results if the second microphone is positioned at least three times (or more) the distance as that between the first microphone and the sound source(s). For example, If you place a microphone 60cm away from a vocalist, the second microphone being used to capture the second vocalist should be at least 180cm away from the first microphone and vice versa.

If you consider sound pressure in the free field and the inverse distance law then sound pressure levels (SPL) decrease by 6dB each time the distance from a given sound source is doubled. Therefore when we relate this to the position of microphones and consider different sounds being summed into mono, if the microphones have enough distance between them then the wanted signal is louder than the unwanted spill and so when they are summed there is less risk of audible artifacts in the sound associated with phase coherence and destructive interference.

The rule of thumb is not a real concern when recording or mixing in stereo. However, a practitioner may look at the distances between the microphones of a time of arrival technique such as a basic spaced AB pair so that the microphones are equidistant from a given sound source.

Again it is about using your ears, and if you are concerned then check your work and monitor in mono from time to time. If there is a noticeable issue with destructive interference then either move a microphone at the source, change the polar response pattern on the microphone (if possible), mute one or more of the microphone channels during post, or consider using a time alignment tool.

Over time practitioners develop their ears and the placement of multiple microphones becomes second nature.

AC Alternating current.

Abffussor Acoustic panel that can be utilised for the diffusion and absorption of sound.

Absorption In the field of audio and acoustics this is when the energy of sound is impacted and changed into a different type of energy. Different materials have varying absorption coefficients, which alter in a value (or percentage) between 0 and 1. The values represent how much a surface material will effectively either reflect or absorb an oncoming sound wave at a given frequency.

Acoustics How a given space/environment impacts sound. Also the field of research concerned with the science of sound.

Active device A device that requires power to operate and utilises integrated circuits, valves (vacuum tubes), transistors. In recording such devices are, for example, often involved with gain staging and amplification.

A/D converter (ADC) A system utilised to convert analogue waveforms into a digital format, namely binary numbers (*see* **Bit depth** and **Sample rate**).

Ambience   The unique acoustical characteristics of an environment or space. It can also be considered in the sense of mood, character, vibe and atmosphere, which is hugely important in crafting a space in which to be creative.

Ambisonics   Arguably based in part, or rather a progression of the principles associated with the Blumlein and MS techniques developed by Alan Blumlein. Ambisonic recording is source point and works via adding and subtracting various differences in level or intensity captured via a tetrahedral microphone (four sub-cardioid capsules mounted to form a tetrahedron). Utilising such an array, the varied polarisation of their diaphragms (A-format) is converted (matrix) to create B-format. B-format utilises a combination of polar response patterns, three figure of eight (bi-directional) patterns and an omni polar response pattern to capture the directionality and amplitude of a given incoming sound source, respectively. The three figure of eight patterns (X, Y, Z) and the omni polar response pattern (W) can be added and subtracted to garner and localise sound cues and sources that can be captured and reproduced in mono, stereo, surround or 3D sound with height cues (periphonic sound).

Ampere (Amp)   Unit of electrical current pertaining to the amount of electricity that flows through a conductor.

Amplifier   A device utilised to increase the level (amplitude) of an electrical signal. It amplifies the current, power or voltage of a given signal (*see* **Gain**).

Amplitude   The level or degree of a given signal, which could, for example, be sound pressure or an electrical signal. The maximum value reached is referred to as the peak amplitude.

Amplitude distortion   Occurs when the shape of a waveform input into a given system is altered by amplification and results in a different output. The change in output does not have to be considered as a change in level, but can be crafted in such a manner that a change in tone and colour occurs (*see* **Harmonic distortion**).

Analogue   The continuous representation or replica of a varying signal, such as a change in sound pressure, being represented by a change in voltage when using a microphone. This is opposed to digital recording, in which a signal is quantised or divided into discrete steps and sampled.

Anechoic   Being without echo or reflections. In terms of a recording studio or the environment in which you are choosing to work, ideally you should avoid such a phenomenon or anything that arguably approaches being considered near anechoic unless you are testing equipment, such as measuring the frequency response of a microphone. An anechoic chamber is a purpose-built room for testing equipment and acoustical measurements. Localisation and the perception of sound would be impacted in a recording or mixing environment that approaches being anechoic.

Articulation   How a note is played and sounds, with a particular focus on how a phrase, passage or event in performance begins and ends.

Attack   The time taken for the initial transient of a given sound or note to reach its peak level (peak amplitude). It can also refer to a control used on input/output amplifiers such as compressors (*see* **Compressor**). The control alters how fast the device responds to applying gain changes and ultimately this can impact the shape of a waveform (*see* **Envelope**).

Attenuate   To reduce the level of a given signal.
Audio frequency   Sometimes referred to as the 'audio spectrum', this covers signals audible within the human hearing range, which is generally

acknowledged as being between 20Hz and 20kHz.

Automation   The ability to write/record parameter changes such as a volume increase, which can then be read back and applied automatically. It can also be set up so that one control, such as a fader on a mixing console, is used to control other parameters or controls on a piece of hardware or within a DAW. One example of such a useful control when recording may be to assign stereo recording or multichannel configurations to one fader so that gain staging can be kept unified when boosting or attenuating a given signal.

Baffle boards   Boards made of various materials with different densities and heights, sometimes referred to 'sound baffles' or more vaguely as acoustic partitions, which can be mounted on castors and positioned to alter room acoustics. More specifically they may be used to enhance isolation or minimise spill within a given recording space. Such devices/studio furniture often have glass panels so that musicians can be partitioned off from one another but retain eye contact. Some boards employ a mixture of materials to provide both sound absorption and diffusion.

Bit depth   In practical terms this directly impacts the resolution of an audio signal in conjunction with the sample rate. The bit depth determines how many values (namely possible amplitude values) can be recorded for each audio sample. The higher the bit depth the better the resolution and in theory the sampled/digital representation of the original analogue signal is more accurate (though as cited in the main text there are exceptions and there may be other technical considerations, such as over-sampling). An increase in bit depth impacts the noise floor of a digital recording. 16-bit provides a dynamic range of 96dB (give or take, depending on the weighting and measurement being

Baffle boards.

used). In essence the bit depth provides the user with a certain amount of amplitude values between 0dBFS (usually the final value at the top of the meter in your chosen DAW) and the noise floor when considering a digital scale. 24-bit, for example, provides the user with 144dB of dynamic range, 32-bit around 192dB and so on, based on around 6dB per bit.

Bleed   When sound bleeds out of headphones into the microphones.

Comb filtering   A phenomenon that occurs as a result of both destructive and constructive interference. It is a form of distortion that occurs when signals/waveforms with the same (or arguably similar) frequencies/spectral content have time differences and are summed together at different points of a given phase shift.

In practical terms, this can be an issue when summing to mono, multiple mono is matrixed together and anywhere signals of similar amplitude and spectral content share the same summed audio output.

One telltale sign of comb filtering occurring is when a summed signal sounds hollow or thin. Here, a good example would be when recording a snare drum with two microphones placed facing each other (above and below the snare) and the polarity has not been inverted on the channel where the microphone is facing upwards below the snare drum.

In extreme situations where a full mix may be summed with a delayed, replica version of itself, such as when a practitioner simultaneously monitors a pre-converter (direct) and post-converter signal via a mixing console, the phenomenon can sound metallic and the noticeable issues pertaining to phase coherence become audibly discernible, and arguably unusable (if not intended as an effect in the first instance).

The distortion is referred to as comb filtering because the summed nulls and peaks that manifest due constructive and deconstructive interference look similar to a hair comb when represented on a linear graph.

Compressor   In the simplest of terms, an 'input/output' amplifier that is used to alter the dynamic range of a signal. Upward compression can be used to bring out aspects of a sound that may have normally decayed away to make a given sound appear larger than life within the listening soundstage, whereas downward compression may simply reduce the peaks of a given signal. Multi-band compressors can be used to focus on particular parts of the frequency spectrum, though many full-band compressors have the ability to filter and therefore only focus on certain areas of the frequency spectrum. Different types of compressors react by attenuating and shaping transients based on various parameters and the circuitry used. This can impact the colour/tone of the sound of a given signal as well as

providing noticeable dynamic changes that can alter the envelope and shape of a sound. Such dynamic changes may be perceived as being more aggressive or adding a subtle cohesion to the given audio in terms of rebalancing spectral content via subtle amplitude changes. You will often hear practitioners referring to such terms as 'punch', 'glue' or 'pumping'. Popular design types of compressors include FET (Field Effect Transistor) models. 'Opto' compressors are electro-optical attenuators in which a light element is used: as the gain fed into the compressor increases, the intensity of the light source increases proportionally. A photoconductive cell is then used to react to the light element and, in the simplest of explanations, reduces the output gain.

Variable gain compressors (Vari-mu) use vacuum tubes (valves) when altering the dynamic range of a given signal. VCA (Voltage Controlled Amplifier) compressors are generally known for being clean, transparent and versatile in terms of the parameters they offer and the way in which compression can be applied.

Other types of compressors to be aware of include devices that utilise pulse width modulation (PWM) and many hybrids that combine different operating principles and electronics. One thing to note is that, whether diodes, transistors, valves or any number and combination of circuits and devices are used to control the flow of electric current, distortion can play a part in helping to craft additional tone. A compressor in short is more than just a tool to alter the dynamic range of a given signal.

Count off   This can be associated with both the sounding of a metronome before recording within a given medium such as a DAW, or the direction of a conductor to provide information about the time signature and tempo to the musicians before they set about performing. Such direction helps with uniformity in terms of timing and can also help with performance articulation.

Critical distance The point at which the direct signal from a given source is equal in SPL to that of the reverberant sound of the same source. Passing this point in one direction and in practical terms would suggest that the sound source you were working with/intending to capture was now more of the reverberant sound than the original direct sound source emanating from a given point within the environment you are working in.

Diffraction A form of distortion created when sound bends around an object present within a given soundfield.

Diffuser Used for sound diffusion.

Diffusion The scattering of sound.

Digital audio workstation (DAW) An application used for recording, editing and mixing, amongst other processes.

Distortion There are many types of distortion. Any time a given signal is altered or deformed in any shape or form it can be considered as a form of distortion. Distortion can be audible in terms of the tone or the perceived image of a sound. Some forms of distortion (*see* **Harmonic distortion**) can be considered as pleasant and effective in making a given sound appear larger than life and exaggerated, among other attributes, whereas others, such as digital/clipping distortion, are frowned upon.

Drop in When a recording artist comes in at a specific part of an arrangement to either overdub or replace a previous recording. Unlike 'punching in', when an engineer may just push record in real time, 'dropping in' often involves the recording musician and engineer finding and deciding on the point to work from.

Dubbing The process by which extra sounds are added to an existing recording. It also pertains to the re-recording or transfer of audio from one format or recording to another.

Dynamics Within the context of recording and mixing music this can be seen as degrees of loudness. More specifically, the dynamic range is the difference between the quietest and loudest parts of a musical performance or passage.

Envelope of sound The shape of a sound or signal, and how such a signal varies over time. In some circumstances, such as when crafting a sound via synthesis, the envelope of a sound can be broken down into the attack, decay, sustain and release (ADSR) times.

Equaliser (EQ) Many different types can be used for corrective and creative practice to sculpt a sound by either cutting or boosting parts of the frequency (audio) spectrum.

Expander The opposite of a compressor, used to expand the dynamic range of a given signal as opposed to reducing it.

Fader A control, normally a slider, either in physical or digital form, that allows the user to alter the level of a given signal.

Filter Normally inductors or capacitors (in physical form) or other electronic components arranged to control the flow of frequencies. Some frequencies are allowed to pass through circuits, while others are attenuated. Active filters allow frequencies to be boosted, whereas passive filters are used for attenuating frequencies.

Gain A reading of how much a given signal is amplified when passing through a circuit (or an emulation of one). Can be used for such considerations as expressing SNR levels, optimising or driving signals, and for adding tone.

Ground loops Sometimes referred to as 'Earth loops'. When two or more electrical devices are wired together and connected in a manner that can provide a potential difference in grounds (specifically voltage differences), it can create a ground loop that manifests as an audible hum. This can be caused by many factors, but one common one is when plugs from different electrical devices in a signal chain are plugged into different mains outlets, or when there are too many grounds. An example might be a synth (plugged into a live room plug socket) interconnected into a mixing console (plugged into a power outlet in the control room) via a Direct Inject (DI) box. One way to rectify this would be to use the ground or 'earth' lift on the DI dox. Where possible, try to plug the devices into the same power outlet. It is also worth checking if any transformers in the power supplies or cables associated with any other pieces of electrical equipment are too close in proximity to the audio signal path.

Harmonic distortion   When a series of existing partials related to a given fundamental (or otherwise), or new partials are increased in level to audibly impact the quality of the sound in question.

Headroom   The space you have to work with or the capacity within a recording or mixing system, such as a DAW or audio converters, before distortion occurs. In a digital system 0dBFS (full scale) is at the very top of a meter and a healthy recording or mix level should peak well below this level.

In an analogue system, if the equipment is calibrated using 0dBu as a reference point (see **Zero level**), then going beyond an optimal point can overmodulate the signal and create interesting tonal changes or distortion. In a digital system this is not the case and you should stay away from 0dBFS, as when digital clipping occurs there are no more '1's and '0's and the result will not sound musical in the way that analogue distortion can.

High pass filter (HPF)   Sometimes referred to as a 'low cut', a high pass filter is used to remove frequencies below a set cut-off point. Some modern tools can provide a gradual cut with a staged cut-off slope or an extreme frequency cut (brickwall).

Impulse response (IR)   The means by which the acoustic properties of a given room or space may be recorded in a reproducible form – a sonic photograph, if you like. Impulse responses are readings that provide such details for a room. Either a fast transient or a burst of sound such as a hand clap can be employed as an impulse to record the reverberation (RT60) time. In order to acquire more sophisticated detail, such as reverberation characteristics and standing waves, a sine sweep can be used. With the latter a sine wave of a constant amplitude is played at a suitable level to generate SPLs to excite the room, sweeping through the audible frequency spectrum from 20Hz up to 20kHz. When the various wavelengths of the different frequencies match that of the room's dimensions or interact in a specific manner, there will be anomalies in the readings. Expressed simply, the amplitude will increase at various frequencies as they naturally react and amplify with the environment or space being measured. Cross-synthesis is used to remove the sine sweep after an IR is captured and what remains is in essence a reading (or possibly a best interpretation) of the acoustic properties of a given room or space. When using the captured IR with a specialist tool such as a convolution reverb, it is then possible to attempt to recreate the reverberation characteristic of the space you initially captured. This can be useful for adding cohesion among other considerations when recording and mixing. Often professionals take many readings of a given space in order to build up a better model of the acoustic properties of the room, space or environment in question.

Reverberation characteristics and other acoustic properties will alter depending on the SPL of a given waveform(s).

Infrasound (infrasonic)   Sound below 20Hz. We may be able to feel its presence, but it is agreed that 20Hz is the lower end of human hearing. Therefore infrasound pertains to sound outside of the human hearing range.

Jam session   Normally, but not always, a creative session between musicians and artists in which ideas can be developed and played out. It may also just serve as a random event when a bunch of players get together, have fun and make music that ends up never being heard or played again.

Kunstkopf   Recording with a synthetic dummy head (binaural recording).

Layering   The process often used in recording and mixing to make the recording or production sound fuller by adding additional layers. When recording a small string or brass ensemble, for example, you may get the performers to play different parts on top of what they have recorded in the first instance to give the listener the impression that more musicians were involved. It can also refer to building or compiling (composite) a musical timbre and sound on a synth by layering various tones or sounds together in an additive manner.

Level (*see also* **Amplitude**) Other than the literal definition, practitioners are on many occasions referring, in a practical sense, to the balance of sounds within a recording or mix when discussing relative levels.

Low pass filter (LPF)   Used to cut off frequencies above a given point (*see* **High pass filter**).

Masking (also referred to as 'frequency' or 'spectral masking')   This is the phenomenon whereby sounds summed together with similar frequencies can lose definition and clarity as one of the given sounds takes precedence within the listening soundstage. In essence, your ability to hear a given frequency or frequencies, which may be integral to the character of a given sound, is reduced as another sound made up of similar frequencies is louder. Extreme masking can blur the sound of

a recording and, or mix on many levels, and can impact the sense of intelligibility, definition, clarity, depth and width within the listening soundstage.

Metering   Devices used to visualise a given reading and provide information about your recording, mix or master. Examples include correlation meters, spectral analysers, spectrograms, and level and loudness meters.

Noise gate   A device used to close an audio pathway down when the signal falls below a given level (set threshold). It is a popular device for reducing noise between takes and a recorded performance when using a tape machine. Also useful for creating effects such as closing down reverberant sound quickly and often in a rhythmic manner via side chaining, editing out unwanted resonance in a given sound and changing the envelope and shape of a sound.

Overdubbing   The process of adding to, or replacing elements of a multitrack recording.

Patchbay   A device used to interconnect the inputs and outputs of various pieces of equipment used for recording and mixing. Usually via bantam jack patch cables, a system of rack-mounted connectors can be used, for example, to parallel (think of this as duplicating) signals for situations such as matrix/decoding the side (difference) channels of an MS stereo recording technique or for inserting a processor (dynamic, spatial, spectral…) into the signal path.

Pre-roll   A set amount of time, nominally defined by bars and beats, before a section of music or an arrangement is focused on for recording. Often in a practical sense, as opposed to a count-off in which the recording artist may only hear a click before entering a period or passage to track or re-record, a pre-roll can be used as well as a cache (to capture detail before the recording kicks in) as an opportunity to play the recording artist a specified number of bars and beats of the music in their headphones so they can play along or prepare before focusing on the part they are performing for the recording. A 'count-off' may be more useful when a musician does not wish to hear any other previously recorded material as it may be off-putting, for example when artists are working with polyrhythms.

Pulse Code Modulation (PCM) The system for converting audio into a series of pulses. Audio is sampled and converted into binary values before being transmitted via the pulses within a digital system.

Punch in & out (recording) Similar to 'dropping in' a musician whilst tracking or overdubbing to focus on a given section of an arrangement or to redress a given error. However, in practice punching 'in' and 'out' is usually associated with a real-time operation whereby the engineer physically pushes and activates the record button in (punching in) and out (punching out) whilst the music is playing. This was common practice when using tape machines and could be a very tricky practice to oversee in terms of capturing the onset of a given sound being tracked. Some may suggest it was an art in its own right, like splicing.

Quadratic diffusor Developed by Manfred R. Schroeder, a QRD is a device made up of a series of different depth wells with the same width and is used to break up and scatter standing waves and primary reflections. Diffusers can be used for corrective and creative purposes, for example when they are attached to baffle boards or similar and placed near to microphones and a given instrument(s) in order to alter the spectral content of what is being captured in relation to the room.

Refraction Another form of sound distortion whereby sound bends and changes direction based on a change in velocity having passed through different mediums. For example, a change

in air temperature would cause refraction of sound waves.

Reverberation Arguably considered at one time as perhaps the most important measurement and characteristic of a given enclosed space. Reverberation pertains to the reflections within an enclosed space that build up almost instantaneously when a given sound source generates sound pressure levels and resultant waveforms that react with the shape, size and materials of a given space. The point where the sound source stops may be expressed in practical terms by measuring the RT60 time, the time it takes for the reverberated sound to lose energy, dissipate or, more specifically, for the sound to decay by 60dB.

Reverberation characteristic This pertains to RT60 times at different frequencies. In essence some enclosed spaces may have longer reverberation times at lower frequencies, while other spaces have them at higher frequencies. Certain spaces can add creative character to a recording and the reverberation characteristic of the space is a major consideration in this context. Reverberation characteristic and other acoustic properties will change depending on the SPL of a given waveform(s).

Sample rate The number of times the analogue to digital converter in either your designated converters or audio interface samples the instantaneous amplitude of an incoming analogue waveform per second.

44.1kHz refers to when 44100 samples (readings) of an analogue signal are taken per second in order to create a digital signal (a discrete representation of the original waveform being sampled)

48kHz (48000 samples taken per second) is commonly used for audiovisual media.

Higher sample rates such as 88.2kHz (88200 samples per second), 96kHz, 176.4kHz and 192kHz (192,000 samples per second) are used for more specialised reasons such as corrective or creative processing, such as pitch shifting. Some location recordists also prefer higher sample rates when recording large orchestras and believe that more detail is captured pertaining to the room acoustics. A more contemporary consideration could be when considering spatial audio, particularly when the listener is not static and moves around, for example in a VR immersive environment.

Separation   The process of trying to minimise spill between various sounds and instruments. Some studios have acoustic panels, baffle boards or multiple live rooms that can be used to separate various instruments and so minimise spill. This provides more control when it comes to processing and balancing the sound(s) within a mix.

Signal to noise ratio (SNR)   In practical terms this is the ratio between the wanted signal and the noise floor. Noise is always present, whether it is electrical or background noise. This is related to gain staging and optimal levels (*see* **Zero level**), but it can be seen as measurement of how much of the desired signal outweighs the noise in question and within the same signal path being shared.

Sound pressure level (SPL)   The measurement of sound intensity. Note that this is different to perceived loudness, which is subjective.

Spill   When a microphone captures the sounds of other instruments or sounds that are not intended for this particular microphone. Spill can be a consideration when recording many different instruments simultaneously or when one instrument is made up of many different elements. An example of the latter would be a drum kit, for which multiple microphones may be used to capture individual parts of the kit. Even with the microphones positioned very close to the snare drum, for example, other elements such as a hi-hat can be captured (or spilled) into the microphone used to capture the snare.

Splice (tape)   The process by which a recording is edited by cutting and rejoining parts of a reel of tape. This is similar to the process of cutting and pasting sections of audio within a modern DAW, albeit requiring far more skill and possibly creating more stress. The tape is cut at different angles depending on the transition of the audio sections being edited. A 'butt' splice, for example, is a cut made at right angles and is mostly used to provide a dead stop and silence.

Standing waves   This is a huge subject to consider in its own right. It can first be considered, for example, as an integral principle when examining how sound is generated by many musical instruments. It can also be approached in terms of how a given enclosed space impacts the resonance of a sound within that space. If the latter approach is considered through the lens of room acoustics, then it pertains to the constructive interference (by boosting a specific frequency and its related set of frequencies, or room modes related to the wavelength and the room dimensions, materials and so on) and destructive interference (by attenuating the same elements) that occur to a given sound wave when they are summed together.

Tape machine (reel to reel)   A recording device based on the principle of electromagnetic induction, which utilises a magnetic field to induce an electrical current. Tape made of specialist material such as Mylar is coated with iron oxide. When this material is passed across the tape heads, the current generated polarises the oxide particles, capturing a reading of the given signal. Tape machines thicken up the lower end of the frequency spectrum, creating dynamic and harmonic distortions that many recording engineers and musicians consider enhance the character of their recordings.

Tie-lines   Used to interconnect a live room to a control room and vice versa. Usually a tie-line, wall box or stage box is used to connect microphones to the mixing console (or outboard) via an XLR

Tie-lines.

cable. Foldback (headphone mix) is sent from the control room to the live room usually via an aux or cue send on the mixing console. The signal is then fed into a headphone amp (or flexible matrix distribution system such as a Furman headphone system) and in turn to sets of headphones or re-amping box in the live room.

Tracking
Another name for recording, normally associated with multitrack recording.

Transient
Initial, short burst of a signal, which is at its highest point in amplitude for that particular sound, or specifically (when analysed) the initial upsurge of a fundamental frequency and its related partials, which is high in amplitude and generally short lived. From the point of human perception this information is vital in determining different types of sounds.

Ultrasound
Sound above the agreed limits of the human hearing range. Technically this is frequencies above 20kHz, though some research has suggested that there are times when people can hear frequencies above this upper limit. It is also a consideration that just because we do not hear such frequencies, that does not mean we do not feel them via other senses. As a result such frequencies can impact the quality and ultimately how the recording is received by the listener.

Unity gain
The process of helping minimise distortion and noise within a given signal chain by preserving and matching the input level to the output level. A 1 volt input, for example, should produce a 1 volt output no matter what is in the chain. In simpler terms, imagine adjusting a plugin's output level in your chosen DAW, such as a compressor, to make sure you came out at the same level you went in with, regardless of any dynamic

processing taking place. A way to check this is to bypass the plugin and see if the output level matches or, in practical terms, is similar to the input level whether the plugin or hardware is active or bypassed. Some practitioners use sine waves for such calibration purposes. Unity gain, if applied when mixing in the box with a DAW, can help preserve a decent amount of headroom on the channel in question.

Valves (tubes)   A valve or 'tube' is an electronic device consisting of anodes and cathodes, types of electrodes, that uses a heater element within a vacuum, hence the description 'vacuum tube'. As a cathode heats up with voltage, the negatively charged electrons get pulled towards the positive anode (plate). Basic diodes are semiconductors: as the electrons only flow one way, they can be used as a rectifier to convert AC into DC (direct current). Triodes that include a 'grid' and other components alongside the anode and cathode can be used as amplifiers. This is a very basic explanation, but the practical result is that recording engineers and musicians will find that using various valves alongside other electronic components, such as transistors and transformers, can impact the tone produced. Some will also argue that components such as valves react differently in terms of feel and performance. Once transducers have been used to convert one source of energy into another, as for example when a microphone converts a change in air pressure (acoustic energy) into voltage (electrical), how that voltage flows through a device depends on the electronic components used.

Velocity of sound   The speed at which a sound propagates through a given medium such as air, particle to particle, as a longitudinal waveform.

Volume unit (VU) meter   Used to measure the average, over time or moment to moment, amplitude of a given signal as opposed to instantaneous peaks. As a physical device it is electromechanical. Some view it as a more natural, if less accurate way – especially at certain frequencies – of indicating amplitude changes during recording and mixing.

Waveform   A representation of the cyclic propagation of a given form of energy over time. When considering sound, a waveform can normally be seen as the visualisation of changes in sound pressure levels in a medium such as air. It can also be a representation of an electrical signal.

Wavefront   In very simple terms, this phenomenon pertains to sound and how we make sense of directionality. A wavefront of an incoming sound can be considered as the point at which multiple sound waves meet up at the ear (the pinna). The brain then localises from where sound is emanating based on differences in phase (time) and amplitude (intensity/level).

Wavelength   The distance one whole cycle of a given frequency covers peak to peak, high pressure (or trough to trough, low pressure). The lower the frequency the longer the wavelength. The higher the frequency the shorter the wavelength. High frequency is considered as being more directional due to the principle that the wavelengths are shorter and do not spread out as much in a given soundfield.

XLR cable   Sometimes referred to as 'cannon' connectors, these are mainly used to convey low level microphone signals. They are balanced cables usually fitted with a three-pin male (pins out) and female connection. More pins or connections may be incorporated if a stereo microphone is being connected or in cases where microphones that utilise multiple diaphragms are configured in a specialist array for working with principles such as ambisonics.

Y-lead   A cable that splits from one type of connector at one end to two at the other and can therefore feed two destinations. Such cables may be used in a mixing console insert point.

Zero level (0dB)   A reference point for optimal signal levels for use on calibrated equipment. A modern reference point of 0dBu matches 775mv, whereas 0dBv, sometimes written as dB(v), equates to 1 volt. On a peak programme meter (PPM) in the United Kingdom, 0dB would produce a reading of 4.

Once we know what we are working with in terms of metering, we can apply gain staging to optimise a given signal. If a signal goes above the optimal level, it can be viewed as overmodulated; if the signal goes below, then conversely a signal can be undermodulated.

Zero return   On a tape machine this is a location point that can be set so that you can easily return to a given starting point of a recording (or mix). It is similar to bar 0 on a timeline of a DAW, but the engineer has to spool the tape onto the machine and let the tape roll to provide some lead-in time and offset before setting a zero return point. This can help to avoid putting fingers on the start of a reel of tape and inadvertently damaging the recording.

INDEX

First published in 2024 by
The Crowood Press Ltd
Ramsbury, Marlborough
Wiltshire SN8 2HR

enquiries@crowood.com

www.crowood.com

British Library Cataloguing-in-Publication Data
A catalogue record for this book is available from the
British Library.

ISBN 978 0 7198 4368 6

Acknowledgements
Although I appreciate this offering only touches
the proverbial surface when it comes to the art
and science of recording, I want to take this
time to say thank you to everyone who has
contributed to this book in one way or another.
Whether a friend, a colleague or both, you have
supported me on many levels and I am eternally
grateful.

I would like to especially thank Josh Diamond
for documenting many of the sessions we have
worked on together over recent years and for
kindly providing some of the photos.

Thank you to engineer, musician and producer
Brendan Lynch for providing me with the opportunity to work from his amazing studio and for allowing me to photograph some of his equipment at Le
Mob studios.

Jason Kristensen and Mike Doyle have always
been there to listen and inspire over the years, as
has Jules Manser my business partner.

I would also like to thank my wife Renata and
two sons Samuel and Theodore, as well as my
brothers and extended family for making me smile
and offering encouragement.

I would like to dedicate the book to my dad
Peter and late mother, Mary Frances Brocklesby,
for always believing in me.

Typeset by Simon and Sons
Cover design by Design Deluxe
Printed and bound in India by Thomson Press Ltd

RELATED TITLES FROM CROWOOD

THE ANALOGUE APPROACH TO DIGITAL RECORDING AND MIXING

Fran Ashcroft

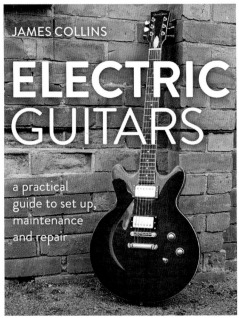

JAMES COLLINS

ELECTRIC GUITARS

a practical guide to set up, maintenance and repair

TEMPLATE MIXING AND MASTERING

THE ULTIMATE GUIDE TO ACHIEVING A PROFESSIONAL SOUND

Featuring the full template used on sixteen No.1 songs!

BILLY DECKER AND SIMON TAYLOR
FOREWORD BY RODNEY ATKINS

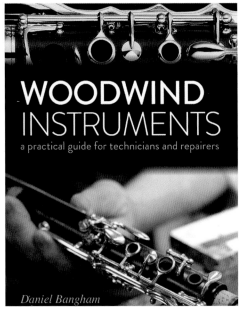

WOODWIND INSTRUMENTS

a practical guide for technicians and repairers

Daniel Bangham